Series
HERITAGE

No 3

ISBN 953-215-307-1

Text
ANTE NAZOR

Translated by
Davor Šovagović

Photographs
Živko Bačić, Patrik Macek, Mladen Katavić, Željko Lukunić,
Branko Ostojić, Ivo Pervan, Andrija Carli, Krešo Strnad
Arhiv Turističke naklade, O-TISAK

Editors
Ana Ivelja-Dalmatin
Davor Nikolić
Mato Njavro
Marija Vranješ
Milan Vukelić

Editor-in-Chief
Mato Njavro

Responsible editor
Ana Ivelja-Dalmatin

Art editor
Milan Vukelić

Publisher
TN Turistička naklada d.o.o., Zagreb

For Publisher
Marija Vranješ

© Copyright by Turistička naklada d.o.o., Zagreb

Photolithographs
Studio DIM, Zagreb

Set and printed by
VJESNIK d.d., Zagreb

Zagreb 2006.

⇦ *The small Romanesque church of St Nicolas not far from Nin, 12th C*

HRVATSKA

The baptistery of the Croatian Prince Višeslav (around 800 A.D.) from Nin

»*Neither hills nor*
valleys, rivers or sea
neither clouds
not even rain or snow
are my Croatia...
because Croatia is not the soil,
stone or water
Croatia is the word which I learned
from my mother
and it means much more than the
word itself;

it links me closer with Croatia,
with Croatia peopled with the
Croats,
their sufferings,
their laughter and their hopes
it links me with the people
and being a Croat, I am the
brother of all people;
wherever I go
Croatia is with me«.

(D. Ivanišević)

CROATIA, A PICTURE OF BEAUTY

This country has been inherited from our ancestors and special care has been taken, for Croatia is a masterpiece made by a perfect artist, nature itself. There are many places of untouched nature, calm and beauty, ranging from lush islands and islets to pearls of architecture in small Dalmatian towns, to the steep and rough but magnificent mountainous Croatia, the picturesque hills of the Zagorje region and the corn fields of Slavonia. The richness of the landscape, its vegetation, relief and geological formations, the various types of flora and fauna and the unique historical and cultural monuments are all found in this relatively small space, as though nature had its inspiration right here creating such an abundance of natural beauty.

Slavonian fields – a granary for Croatia

»*The glorious one*« say the Croats about their country, dedicating the first line of their anthem to its beauty, praising the bravery and glory of their anscestors in the battles against their conquerors. An unlucky history of defensive wars, forced the Croats to be alert and to hold a sword in their hands. However, Croatian history is mostly creative. Even when Croatians were bleeding and were expelled from their homes, they were at the same time building, painting, writing, printing and dreaming about their freedom. The Croatian anthem of freedom was written by one of the most famous Croatian poets, called Ivan Gundulić from Dubrovnik who describes the relationship between the Croats and the treasure of freedom:

> *»Oh how nice, how dear and sweet*
> *the freedom is,*
> *the gift that Allmighty God gave us,*
> *the cause of truth and all our glory*
> *the only adornment of this Dubrava,*
> *neither all the silver and gold nor*
> *the human lives*
> *can match your pure beauty!«.*

The word »Libertas« means freedom and it is marked on the flag of the Republic of Dubrovnik as a symbol of life and the only thing which is worth living for. It was a constant inspiration for the Croats who for centuries have fought for their existence. The carved inscription on the Tower of Lovrijenac warns all those who might forget what is most precious for dignified people:

> *»Freedom is not for sale for all the gold«*
> *(Non bene pro toto libertas venditur auro).*

⇦ *Zagreb – a city of a specific atmosphere and spirit*

The picturesque flow of the beautiful Zrmanja River

Paklina Islands – Beauty of the Hvar coves

A winter idyll in the Zagorje hills

The canyon of the Paklenica – full of geo-morphological riches

Zavratnica Bay – a geo-morphological monument to nature

Velika Mlaka – one of the most beautiful venues of the Turopolje wooden sacred architecture

⇦ *Šarengrad Ada – am area of preserved woods and the power of the Danube*

The Natural Park Kopački rit in Baranja

Gorski kotar – a harmony of woods and fresh waters

"God, give us a big sun and small bura" ⇨

The fertile valley of the Neretva River

CROATIA, A LAND FROM PRIMORDIAL TIMES

*A*ccording to the Constitution, the Republic of Croatia is a unique, unseparable, democratic and social state, where the government functions through the delegation of people and belongs to the people as a union of free and legally equal citizens.

All citizens are equal and have the same rights regardless of race, faith, nationality, social status and political orientation. The legal and governmental tradition dates from the period of medieval principalities and kingdoms and was confirmed on the 22nd of May, 1992. when Croatia was elected as a member of the OUN.

The Republic of Croatia is divided into administrative regions. The ruling power is divided between the legislature, executive and judiciary.

It is applied through the Parliament which was founded on the semi-presidential system. The Croatian parliament (Sabor) is a one-house parliament (the House of Representatives) that makes the laws.

The state symbols are the red, white and blue flag with a coat of arms based on the Croatian historical bearings and the national anthem called »Our beautiful homeland«. The official currency is kuna (1 kn has 100 lipa). The capital is Zagreb.

In 2001 there were 4.437,460 inhabitants (approximately 78,5 inhabitants per square kilometer). The majority of the inhabitants are located near urban centers. Out of this number, 89,63% are Croats (3.977,171) and 2.01% are national minorities.

Croatia is a Central European, Panonian and Mediterranean country and at the same time, it is a mountainaous, lowland, littoral and continental country.

The diversity of the country is itensified by its natural beauty. It is shaped like a horse-shoe and in the geographical sense, it is divided into the Pannonian and the Peripannonian Croatia (eastern or central Croatia) and the mountainous and Mediterranean (littoral) Croatia.

The total surface area of Croatia is about 89,988 square kilometers (the mainland - 56,538

Vineyards in stone

⇐ *The flow of the Cetina River*

Picturesque landscape of Međimurje

square kilometers, the sea - about 33,450 square kilometers).

The mainland borders are 2,028 km long; it borders on Slovenia with 501 km (24,7%), Hungary 329 km (16.2%), Serbia 241 km (11.9%), Montenegro 2.5 km (1.2%) and Bosnia and Herzegovina 932 km (46%).

The most northern point of Croatia is Žabnik, the community of Sveti Martin on the Mura river (at 46.33'10"N degrees latitude and at 16.22'30"E degrees longitude); the most southern point is the island of Galijula part of the community of Lastovo in the Adriatic sea (at 42.22'40"N latitudue and 16.20'40"E longitude) whilst the most southern point on the mainland is cape Oštro on Prevlaka (at 42.23'30" N degrees latitude and 18.32'E longitude); the most western point of Croatia is Cape Lako, part of the

Lim Bay, one of the most beautiful natural riches of the Istrian peninsula

community of Umag (at 45.29'10'N latitude and 13.29'40E longitude) and the most eastern point is Radevac, near Ilok in Srijem (at 45.11"50"N and 19.27'E longitude).

According to its height, 52.8% of the surface of Croatia is up to 200 m above sea level, 25.6°/a is between 200 and 500 m above sea level, 17.7 % is between 500 and 1000 m high above the sea level, 3.7% is between 1000 and 1500 m above sea level whilst only 0.2%. of its teritory is between 1500 and 2000 m above sea level.

The Dinaric Alps dominate Croatia to the west and the south whilst the mountains between the Sava and the Drava rivers to the north are part of the Dinaric chain but of an earlier origin with lots of karst formations, extending in parallel with the Adriatic coast in the direction of the north-west and the south-east.

CLIMATIC VARIETY

*T*he largest part of Croatia (its eastern and central part and the area of the northern Adriatic) has a mild continental climate with an average temperature of zero degree C in January to 22 degrees C in July, especially in the flat areas.

The coldest parts of Croatia are the areas of Lika and Gorski Kotar with a mountainous climate and an average annual temperature of 8 to 10 degrees C (ranging in winter from minus 2 to minus 4 degrees C on the smaller heights and from 2 to 4 degrees C on the highest peaks of the Dinara mountain chain (ranging in winter from minus 4 to minus 6 degrees C).

In the coastal area and south of the island of Rab, the Mediterranean type of climate prevails i.e, a mild climate, (in January it never falls bellow 5 degrees C) with a short winter period and with long, sunny and warm days in summer (the average temperature in July never exceeds 24 degrees C). Minor daily temperature oscillations and

Brela – Sea, strand, stone and pine trees

Zavižan on the Velebit, a special botanic reserve

a large number of sunny days (up to 2500 hours of annual insolation) have a favourable effect on the human body.

The longest insolation is experienced on the central part of the coast, on the sunny island of Hvar with 2715 hours of annual insolation. The medieval writer Fusko described in one sentence the climate of this area: *Here there is an eternal spring and summer in the most peculiar months«.*

The main winds in Croatia are the *jugo* (a warm and moist south eastern wind, with a speed of 100 km p/h) and the *bora* a cold and gustly north eas-

ten with a speed of up to 150 km p/h. Winds in winter are more severe on the coast than on the mainland, especially the *bora* which can sometimes turn into a hurricane.

Various geological features and specific climatic elements influence the diversity of soil throughout Croatia.

The area of the Sava and the Drava rivers are characterized by moors with flooded, aluvial and fertile soil. The limestone and dolomite mountains are characterized by karst formations with patches of red soil.

FLORA AND FAUNA

*I*n Croatia there is a rich and versatile flora with about 3800 plant species. There are quite a few unique species, particularly those originating from the Velebit and the Biokovo mountains, as well as in the Kvamer area and the island of Vis.

The rich fauna is determined mainly by area, i. e. there are animals belonging to the Mediterranean area and those that can be found on the continent of Europe. Croatia has its own breed of dogs including the Croatian herding dog, the Dalmatian dog, the gun dogs from Posavina and Istria and horses from the area of Međimurje, Posavina and Istria.

Croatia is especially rich in species which are now rare in Europe such as bears, wolves, rix, chamonix, eagles and the almost extinct white-headed vulture. Croatia also possesses a unique species of seal that used to live near the Biševo cave. However, since the seal has not been seen for quite a long time, it is possible that it is extinct.

In the subterranean karst rivers unique species of fish live that are only found in Croatia.

Forests are the natural wealth of Croatia, spreading over 20,630 square kilometers which is about 36.5% out of the total area of Croatia. The forests consist of a large number of different types of trees (seventeen along the coast and fifty-one in the continental part of Croatia). The mountains are rich in forests and and the area of Slavonia is wooded with highly-desirable oak trees. The largest parts of the wooded flat areas are along the Sava river, East of Županja (the area of Spačva), the area of Podravina down to Belišće and the central part of Posavlje - from the Kupčina forest to Prašnik, near Okučani. The most well-preserved forests in the flat areas are those in the natural wildlife parks of of Lonjsko polje and Kopački rit.

Croatia also has its own praries such as the Čorkova valley, which is a special wooded area spreading over 75 hectars. In the northwestern part of the valley/country, are the Plitivice Lakes while Crna Draga is situated between the White and Samarski rocks at the Velika Kapela pass. Among other naturally wooded areas, there is Velika Plješivica - Drenovača with 156.84 hectars, in the community of Donji Lapac, Velika Plješivica Javornik - Tisov vrh with 122.55 hectars, in the community of Korenica and the surroundings of Zagreb etc. (see under »the towns«) and the well-preserved forests such as Laudon's gaj which is situated in the Krbava field (33 hectars) and the area of Tepec-Palačnik-Stražnik (150.15 hectars located on the way from Zagreb to Samobor).

Croatia also possesses botanical and ecological wonders such as the dunes on the island of Rab (Lopar), the island of Mljet (Saplunara) and the Đurđevački peski (Sands from Đurđevo) in Podravina (also called the Đurđevac prairie or the Sahara). The country imposes high standards of environmental protection through the implementation of adequate laws and independent monitoring by professional institutions and non-governmental organisations.

Istrian bovine "boškarin"

Storks arrive in the Natural Park Lonjsko polje every spring

Protected brown bear

Rosemary and pomegranate, botanical specificities of the Adriatic

Čorkova uvala, the most beautiful virgin ⇨ wood of the Dinarides in the National Park Plitvice Lakes

Olive and fig trees, favourite plants of the Mediterranean ambience

Šibenik, "Krešimir's Town"

HISTORICAL EXISTENCE THROUGH THE MILLENIUM

Liberi sumus, non mancipia! (We are free and we are not the slaves)

»We, as the law says, joined the Hungarian side but we are not their subjects. We used to have our own kings and not the Hungarian ones. We did not join the Hungarians by force or through slavery but by our own free will. We did not join their kingdom but rather their king. We are free and we are not slaves.« (A speech addressed to Carl III on March 15, 1712 by the Croatian Parliament).

The origin of the Croats and their settlement in this area has not yet been clarified as data is scarce or doubtful. Some historians believe that the Croats originate far from their country, from the area of Ancient Persia (the present-day Iran). Historians believe that they may have moved westward and settled the Slavic area where they founded their own state called »the white Croatia«. These original Croats forced the Slavs to use their name but gradually they accepted Slavic culture and their language. However the majority of historians consider the so-called Iranian theory unreliable.

The Byzantine emperor Constantine VII Porphyrogenitus (905 -959) wrote a handbook on government entitled »On the Administration of the Empire« (De administrando imperio) where he testifies to the earliest history of the Croats, i.e. their arrival to the present day area. Based on archeological findings and written documents, it is believed that in the seventh century, they settled the area between the Cetina and Zrmanja rivers and the mountainous inland region of Lika and Krbava which is considered the cradle of the Croatian state. In the Middle Ages, the Croats settled the area up to the Drava river, the larger part of Istria and the present state of Bosnia and Herzegovina. They also settled the area of Srijem and Boka Kotarska which form part of the present state of Serbia and Montenegro. Historians mention the first type of governmental organisations such as the Coastal, White or Dalmatian Croatia and the Panonnian Croatia, originally called »Slovinje« (Slavonija).

Gregor from Bar (the friar Duk1janin from the twelfth century) speaks of two parts of the coastal Croatia the White one (from Duvno and Tomislavgrad to Vinodol) and the Red one (from Duvno to Bambalone, in Albania), while the Emperor

Tiny early Croatian church of St Cross in Nin, 9th C

Pluteus from the small church of St Sunday, 11th C, a detail, Escape into Egypt

Constatntine VII Porphyrogenitus, used the term »Pagonia«, Zahumlje, Travunia, Konavle and Duklja, instead of Red Croatia.

Since the Roman times and up until the present day (The Dayton Agreement, 1995), the area settled by the Croats has witnessed empires that were divided, different civilisations existing and many interest that were in constant conflict. Numerous wars were fought and different religions, cultures and inhabitants co-habitated. Consequently the ethnic structure of the area inhabited by the Croats and the boundaries of the Croatian state have changed over the past centuries.

Croatia in the period of the populistic rulers (up to 1102 y.)

Late in the ninth century, during the reign of King Trpimir, King Domagoj and especially King Branimir, Croatia possessed the characteristics of a modern European state. It became an independent duchy, which had a significant political and economical impact on the future Croatian state established on the Adriatic. Economic development and the spread of Christianization were the main factors influencing the creation of the Croatian state. Christianity was spreading among the Croats from different centres including Rome, Aquillea and from the Byzantine towns on the Dalmatian coast. Christianity was also spread by the Franks' and the Byzantine missionaries aswell as the Slavic missionaries and the Saints Cyril and Methodius (in the last quarter of the ninth century).

The Christianization of the local inhabitants led them to develop under the Croatian name their own Christian civilisation. However, up until the tenth century the Pope himself and foreign historians used to call the Croats Slavs.

Figure of a Croatian dignitary, 11th C, Biskupija near Knin

Up until that period, the Croats had not been successful in settling down in the coastal towns of Kotor, Dubrovnik, Split, Trogir and Zadar and on some of the islands such as the island of Rab, Osor and the sland of Krk which were under the Byzantine rule.

King Tomislav (around 910-928) was the first Croatian ruler whom the Pope addressed as a king (rex). The historical sources mention the huge military force of the former Croatian state, including the victory of the king Tomislav over the Hungarians and the powerful army of the Emperor Simeon (893-927). King Tomislav spread his power to the area between the Sava and the Drava rivers and the content of the Pope's letter to his »beloved son Tomislav« hints to the fact that the Croatian ruler had some influence on the Dalmatian towns.

Gable with the name of the Croatian prince Muncimir, 895 A.D.

A unique church organisation was established in 925 and 928 in Split for the whole area of Croatia and Dalmatia, thus accelerating the integration of Dalmatian towns into the Croatian state.

The reign of Petar Krešimir IV (1058-1074) and Dmitar Zvonimir (around 1075-1089) is the most glorious period of the Croatian early medieval period. The area between the Drava river and the Adriatic sea became a single state »The kingdom of Dalmatia and Croatia« (Croatiae Dalmatieque regnum) »which All mighty God spread from the mainland »to our Dalmatian sea« (nostro Dalmatico mari) as the king Krešimir IV called it. The traditional saying goes: »*During the reign of the good ruler Zvonimir all the country was cheerful*

because it was rich and the towns were aboundant in silver and gold«.

The Croats accept the reign of foreign rulers

In 1102 Croatia joined in a personal union with the Hungarian kingdom because the Croats »*according to their own will*« acknowledged the Hungarian King Coloman from the Arpadian dynasty as their own king. The soverignity of Croatia was reflected through the instititutions of the Ban (the Civil Viceroy) and the Parliament (the Sabor). The Arpadians had no influence in the area south of Gvozd. The union had a favourable impact on the development of the nobility and the towns on the eastern part of the Adriatic.

From the twelfth to the thirteenth century, in the area stretching from Istria to Kotor there was a unique system of medieval communes with an urban style of life and artistic achievements which enriched the Croatian culture. In the thirteenth century, a number of »free king's towns« were founded in the interior of Croatia for defensive purposes.

From the thirteenth century on, Slavonia was considered a separate »kingdom« spreading between the Gvozd mountain, the Drava river and along the Una, the Vrbas and the Bosna rivers. Croatia was the called »the kingdom of Croatia, Dalmatia and Slavonia« but outside these political borders, Croats also lived in Istria and on the Dinarides i.e. the area of the medieval Bosnia which was linked with the Croatian territory. The Drina river was a boundary line for centuries between the Western and Eastern civilizations.

The reign of the Croatian and the Hungarian kings in the area south of the Gvozd was of a no-

Monument to the first Croatian King Tomislav

minal nature until the reign of the Anjou kings (Carl Robert I, Ludovic I who was placed on the throne with the aid of the Croatian nobleman Pavao I. Šubić (from Bribir). Ludovic I, the Great (1342 - 1382) crushed the resistance of the Croatian noblemen and according to the »Treaty of Zadar« (1358) he forced Venice to remove their military forces from all Dalmatian towns and islands i.e. »from half of the Kvarner Bay down to Drac«. Thus, the entire Croatian territory from the Drava river to the Adriatic was under the rule of a single ruler, ensuring the prosperity of the Dalmatian towns for half a century. The turbulent times of the Croatian history began in the fifteenth and in the sixteenth centuries. The consequences of the Venetian and the Ottoman invasions were

disastrous, especially the defensive battles against the Ottomans which lasted for centuries (from the fifteenth to the eighteenth century). These battles resulted in numerous Croatian victims and the Croats lost a great part of their territory (mostly in present-day Bosnia and Herzegovina). The area along the Sava, the Vrbas and the Una rivers settled by the Muslims and the Balkan's Vlasi was named the Ottoman's Croatia.

In the year 1493, the Croats were defeated by the Ottomans in the battle on the Krbava field near Udbine. The friar Martinac, the Czech writer reported from Zadar just after the battle *»in the country of the Croats there is such a grief and a lot of tears which/that can break anybody's heart«*. Due to the number of Croat victims and their willingness

Mighty medieval Fort Nehaj on the mount of Saint Saviour above Knin

to defend their homes and Western Europe against the Ottoman invaders, Pope Leon X (1522) called Croatia the *»defensive wall of Christianity«* (antemurale christianitatis). A witness to the Krbava battle, Duke Bernardin Frankopan from Ozalj (1453-1529) delivered a speech on the imperial meeting in Nuemberg/Nuremburg (on November 19, 1522) *»I have come here, your high dukes and highly-esteemed Sirs in order to give you a report on a dangerous peril that threatens us all from the Ottomans, primarily to Croatia and then to your countries, reminding you that Croatia is a shield and a gate of Christianity Therefore, I plead you, on behalf of Croatia and Christianity itself to extend your help to this country which alone defends us from the Ottomans' invasions since the fall of Istanbul (1453). One should be alert to the Ottomans who have become too aggressive. I am saying this with tears in my eyes, stressing that this ferocious enemy of ours destroyed more than a hundred towns and they committed abominable crimes in our country which I had to watch with my own eyes. Just have in mind how much despair they would cause in the Christian world if Croatia succumbed. »IT SHOULD BE YOUR CONCERN AS WELL, IF THE NEIGHBOROUGH'S HOUSE IS ON FIRE.*

When King Ludovic II died in the battle of Mohac in Hungary in 1526, the Croatian and the Hungarian throne became vacant and the Croatian gentry according to their free will elected Ferdinand of Habsburg as their king, at a meeting in Cetingrad on January 1, 1527 with an obligation to defend the country from the Ottomans. Part of the Croatian gentry refused to acknowledge Ferdinand as king provoking a struggle for the Croatian

Remnants of the ancient Fort Prozor above Vrlika

crown. In 1538 Ivan Zapolja acknowledged Ferdinand's rights over Slavonia and Croatia with Dalmatia. At that time, the Croatian territory was divided between Austria, the Ottoman empire and Venice. Along with the Ottoman's invasions of the Croatian territory, the Balkan Vlasis, who were mainly of the Orthodox faith, settled the area.

The Ottoman invasions were followed by refugees moving westward and their Serbian Orthodox faith. The same boundaries set up by the Ottoman invasions served as a blueprint for later Serbian aspirations to create »Greater Serbia«. Besides the Ottomans, the court of Vienna, due to its inability to cover the costs of paid soldiers, encouraged the settlement of the Vlasi in order to defend the boundaries. On a newly created military boundary, the deserted Croatian territory was left over, serving as a protection zone. In the

sixteenth century, the Croatian political territory was reduced to pieces with a defence line on the Kupa river. The crucial moment for the survival of the Croatian kingdom was the battle near the Sisak tower on June 22, 1593 when about 4,500 Christian soldiers (mostly Croats) defeated the superior Ottoman power. The Croats were led by the civil viceroy Tomas Erdöedy. Since the Court in Vienna made peace with the Ottomans instead of helping to defend the Croatian and the Hungarian territory, their noblemen tried to oppose Vienna but it was all in vain. The leaders of the Croatian noblemen Petar Zrinski and Fran Krsto Frankopan were executed in 1671 in Novo Mesto near Vienna. They died as heroic victims fighting for freedom. In memory to Zrinski and Frankopan, there is an old saying *A man lives forevever if he dies in an honest way!*

Tvrđa – the oldest part of Osijek

31

Old town of Sisak, a unique example of the defensive architecture

Monumental Fort Nehaj rises above the town of Senj

Slavonski Brod, a fort from the 18th C

After the Ottomans had tried to conquer Vienna for the last time in 1683, the great liberation war started and a large number of the Croats participated in it. The peace treaty signed in Sremski Karlovci, enabled the Croats to regain their former territory up to the Una river, the southern part of the Velebit and Slavonia (between the Drava and the Sava rivers), except for the southeastern part of Srijem with Zemun and Mitrovica. To the South, the local people in collaboration with the Venetians took over the area of Knin, Vrlika, Sinj, Vrgorac and Gabela, known as Dalmatia, from the Ottomans. On the request of the citizens of Dubrovnik, some passages were left free in the area of Klek (Neum) and Sutorine for the Ottomans to reach the sea, in order to prevent the Venetians from sharing the border with the Republic of Dubrovnik. Those corridors served only as a separation line and not as a real exit to the sea. According to the peace treaty signed in Belgrade (1739), the Sava river was a frontier with the Ottoman empire, while the present-day frontiers of the Republic of Croatia were set up mainly by the treaty in Svištovo between Leopold II and sultan Selim III.

Up until the eighteenth century, 1,600.000 Croats were killed, expatriated or were taken as slaves. Many Croats settled in Austria (called the Croats from Gradišće), in Italy (those from Moliš), then in Hungary, Slovakia, the Czech Republic and in western Romania. These were the most severe consequences of the wars against the Ottomans.

Croatian national revival

The centralistic reign of Maria Theresa (1740-1780) and her son Joseph II jeopardized the independence of the Croatian parliament (Sabor). This was the period when the medieval feudal system was in its final stages. The French Revolution in 1789 abolished the feudal system and enabled the development of nationalistic states in Europe. The ideals of the French civil revolution reached Croatia, which was on the margins of Europe at that time, i,e, on the border between Christianity and Islam. It seemed that reformers like J. Drašković, Lj. Gaj, I. Kukuljević Sakcinski, J. Jelačić, I. Mažuranić and others would never be able to reject foreign ideas on the arrangement of the state. However, their faith and persistence, despite the fact that »we never had our own kings« helped them to organize the national revival movement called the Illyrian revival. The national identity was based on the history and tradition of a cultural identity. In that period,

Krapina – monument to Ljudevit Gaj, a writer and Illyrian revival scholar

Zagreb – Ban Josip Jelačić on the horse

our own language, based on the widely spread stokavian dialect and on the highly reputable literature from Dubrovnik, was created along with the orthography and the »gajica« alphabet. The first reading rooms, libraries, theatres etc. were also opened.

During the reign of the Civil Viceroy Josip Jelačić (1848) the main aims of the movement were fullfilled. The Croatian government (the governor's council) was established, servitude was abolished and the first civil parliament was summoned. The largest part of the territory was united under the reign of the Croatian governor. The ideals of the Croatian national revival spread throughout Croatia and even outside its borders in

Bačka, Bosnia, Boka Kotorska and partly in Austria.

World War I and World War Il

During World War I, Croatia formed part of the Austria-Hungary monarchy. Some Croatian politicians who could not accept such a situation (A. Trumbić, F. Supilo, I. Meštrović), were active abroad through the Croatian and later through the Yugoslav committee raising funds and recruiting volunteers to fight on behalf of the Antante. By the end of the war, on October 29, 1918, the Croatian parliament broke all statal state and legal links with the Austro-Hungarian Empire and proclaimed »the national and independent state of the

Ancient hill-fort at Trsat with a magnificent view to Rijeka and Kvarner

Slovenians, Croats and Serbs« (SHS) in the area which was within the Austrian-Hungary monarchy (down to the Drina river and Zemun). The Serbian Prime Minister N. Pašić signed the agreement in Geneva, on November 19,1918, certifing the existance of the state of the Slovenians, Croats and Serbs (SHS) as a separate territory with all legal and autonomous functions until a new constititution was passed. Because of their aspirations for Croatian territory (Dalmatia and Slavonia) and for Bosnia and Herzegovina which were, according to the London treaty from 1915, indirectly guaranteed to the Serbs, the Serbian government never respected the signed document.

Political circumstances and the Croat fear that their territory would be divided between Italy and Serbia, forced them to sign in Belgrade on December 1, 1918 the union with the kingdom of Serbia. Although the Croatian parliament never approved it, the Kingodom of the Serbs, Croats and Slovenes was established and in 1929 it was proclaimed the Kingdom of Yugoslavia. Bloody demostrations held on December 1, 1918 on the Jelačić square in Zagreb, known as »the December victims« against the union, showed what a newly-created state was going to be like. In 1928 the Croatian delegates were wounded and the leader of the Croatian Peasant's Party Stjepan Radić was assasinated in the National Assembly in Belgrade. The centralized and the unitarian government, the Serbian terror, the unsolved Croatian question as well as the jeopardized Croatian identity were

Island of Palagruža, the kingdom of sea-gulls, a paradise for fishermen and boaters

the reason for the Croats' disagreement with the so-called First Yugoslavia. The negligence of the Serbian policy concerning the Croatian territory was reflected in the fact that Serbia left a part of the Croatian territory to Italy (Istria, Rijeka, the islands of Cres, Lošinj, Zadar, Palagruža etc.)

There were attempts in 1939 to solve the Croatian question by the creation of the Governor's province of Croatia which encompassed the area of the present Croatian territory (except the territory under the Italian rule), i.e. Bosanska Posavina (the area along the Sava river in Bosnia), the central part of Bosnia, western Herzegovina and the community of Šid, now in Serbia and Montenegro. At the same time, the Serbs established the »Krajina« movement in the very center of Zagreb,

rejecting the idea of creating any Croatian association in order to implement the Serbian policy. In cooperation with military circles in Belgrade and with the Serbian Orthodox church, they requested that a part of the Croatian territory be joined to the Serbian one (the same scenario repeated in 1991). The formation of Croatian governmental institutions within Yugoslavia stopped at the beginning of the World War II.

Due to the clumsy policies of Croatian politicians which divided the Croats, the period of the World War II was the most tragic one in the history of Croatia. The Independent State of Croatia was proclaimed with reliance upon the fascist forces and with their favour, part of the Croatian territory was handed over to them. Under their non-democratic rule (the ignorance of the parliament, the formation of the concentration camps and the murder of those who did not share the same opinion) the aspirations of the Croatian people could not be fulfilled. The majority of the Croats were against the division of their country and against the totalitaristic policies of the Nazis. Moreover, the first anti-fasicst brigade in the former Yugoslavia was founded on June 22, 1941 by the Croats. Compared with other anti-fascist movements created in Europe, the proportion of the Croats in the anti-fascist movement during World War II was rather significant. This enabled Croatia to become a part of the victorious anti-fascist coalition.

By the end of the World War II, a bloody tragedy called »the Crucifix path« happened in Bleiburg where the partisans killed thousands of civilians and soldiers of the Independent State of Croatia who were handed to the partisans by the Allies. Being skillfull in diplomacy and hiding the historical facts, the Serbs credited themselves with the antifascist struggle, creating the prerequisites for the usurpation of Vojvodina with part of the Srijem area and the Boka Kotarska bay.

From the legal point of view, Croatia had, in the so-called Second Yugoslavia (the Federative People's Republic of Yugoslavia and the Socialist Federative Republic of Yugoslavia), the characteristics of a state within the federation of the Yugoslav republics and it was basically sovereign in relation to the federation and its government. The totalitarian federative system did not function in practice. The Croats issued »A Declaration on the name and the position of the Croatian literary language« in 1967 demanding the equal rights for all languages spoken in Yugoslavia. Aspirations to overwhelm the totalitarian and unitarian Yugoslav regime turned in 1971 into a national movement called »the Croatian spring« which demanded economic reform and democratization of the country etc. The movement was put down in December, 1971 causing arrests and persecutions of the Croats, forcing many of them to emigrate abroad.

As a consequence of »the Croatian spring movement«, the new Yugoslav constitution was passed in 1974, containing the elements of confederation within the system of the federal government. The Constitution of the Republic of Croatia stressed the fact that the Croatian people established its state called The Socialist Republic of Croatia based on the right for its separation and unification with other peoples according to their own wish. In the days to come and with the aggression of Serbia on Croatia in 1991, this fact helped Croatia in its recognition as an independent state.

The Homeland War

After the fall of the Berlin wall in 1989, the Croats as well as many other Europeans, rejected communism at multi-party elections in 1990. After refusing to acknowledge the democratically elected government in Croatia and to accept any kind of reform in Yugoslavia, the Serbs, backed up by the Yugoslav Army and the Chetnics, attacked mercilessly and conquered almost one third of the whole Croatian territory. The Serbian aggression on Croatia in 1991 and on Bosnia and Herzegovina in 1992 was the most dreadful event in Europe since World War II.

In spite of all this, Croatia was not conquered. The Serbian superiority in terms of quantity of weapons and military force, was overpowered by the bravery and skill of the Croatian soldiers. The hundred-year old dream of a »Greater Serbia«

Vukovar, winter port and the estuary of the Vuka to the Danube

went downhill along with the idea of the Viroviti-ca-Karlovac-Karlobag western frontier, although the towns like Vukovar, Vinkovci, Osijek, Karlovac, Sunja, Gospić, Zadar, Šibenik, Dubrovnik and others suffered the consequences of the war severely. On January 15, 1992, Croatia was recognized by the European states and on May 22 it became a permanent member of the OUN. A two-day visit by Pope Paul II to Zagreb on September 10, 1994 was rather symbolic. The whole of Croatia together with the Holy Father prayed for peace in Croatia and Bosnia and Herzegovina.

In a short period of time, a modern army was formed, based on the expertly trained professional brigades. The military success of the Croatian army and the police surprised both the enemy and military analysts. By the end of 1995, the Croats had conducted brillant military actions and liberated a large part of its territory thus ensuring the repossession of the occupied parts of Eastern Slavonia. The Dayton Agreement of 1995 stopped the war in Croatia and in Bosnia and Herzegovina. The Croats created their own state despite the huge number of victims and enormous material damages. When the war stopped there were no longer any more obstacles for the further development of democracy in Croatia and its reorganization into a modern state, i.e. a state of justice and abundance for all its citizens.

CULTURAL HERITAGE

*D*uring its history Croatia has always been up-to-date with European cultural trends and quite a number of Croatian scientists and artists contributed significantly to the development of European and global science and culture. All artistic styles known in Europe are more or less represented in Croatia. Certain original regional styles in architecture and sculpture evidenced by the old Croatian churches are also evident. Croatian art and literature is largely connected with the Europeans and is represented in the old town communes from the fifthteen century on. These town communes were situated along the coast and in the so-called »free towns« in the continental part of Croatia. The pearls of the Croatian cultural heritage- the old towns of Dubrovnik, Trogir, the Diocletian's palace in Split, as well as the Euphrasias' basilica in Poreč are all included in the UNESCO's list of the World's cultural heritage.

Famous Vučedol she-pigeon, a clay vessel in the shape of a bird, 3rd millennium B.C.

There are valuable artefacts dating even from the prehistoric times. A representative example is an encrusted hollowware from Vučedol near Vukovar, the so-called »dove from Vučedol« (about 2800 B.C.) which is dear to the Croats, especially after the tragic fall of Vukovar during the Homeland war in 1991.

Before the arrival of the Croats, the whole area was under the influence of the Greek, Roman and Byzantine culture. Monuments from the Roman times are of a particular interest such as the Arena and the Sergijev's Arch in Pula, the Diocletian's palace in Split, the ruins of Salona and the aquaduct near Split (still in use nowdays), the sensational findings of the imperial statues from Augusteum in Narona (Vid near Metković) and other monuments. The Euphrasias' basilica in Poreč with its famous mosaics dating from the sixth century is a masterpiece of Byzantine art.

The old Croatian pre-Romanesque period is characterized by the findings from necropolis such as the metal earings, the inscriptions carved in stone, the unique small churches with domes dating from the ninth to the eleventh century (St. Crucifix in Nin, St. Peter's in Priko near Omiš, St. Lovro in Zadar, some small churches on the islands of Krk, Brač, Lopud and Šipan with the church furniture (the baptismal font of Duke Višeslav, parts of the altars with inscriptions and diplomatic documents.

There are also some representative examples of the Romanesque architecture such as the cathedrals along the coast (those with belltowers on the island of Rab, in Osor, Trogir, Zadar etc.). In the Croatian Srijem there are some well-preserved

Dubrovnik, a City unique among the cities of the world

Trogir, old town, the splendour of centuries

Split, Egyptian sphinx at Peristil with the face of Tutmosis III (1468-1436 B.C.)

⇐ *Split, the city within the Diocletian Palace*

Split, interior of the early Croatian church of St Martin at the Golden Gate

Split, Peristil, the central open area framed with monumental columns

⇦ *The cathedral of St Duje, a symbol of Split
and the most beautiful part of the Imperial
Palace*

Famous Split quay

Interior of the cathedral of St Duje, harmony and beauty

Bas-relief of the Flagellation of Christ on the sarcophagus of St Staš, the work of Juraj Dalmatinac, 1448, in the Split cathedral

Bas-relief on the doorframe of the Split cathedral, the work of Master Buvina, 1214

Remnants of the amphitheatre of the ancient Salona, previously a rich Adriatic town

Romanesque churches (Morović) or their parts in Bapska, Stari Mikanovci. In the continental part of Croatia, there were many Romanesque buildings that were destroyed by the Tartars in 1242.

The Romanesque period of Croatian art is characterized by the exceptional works of art such as the carved doorway of the Cathedral in Split made by Andrija Buvina and the monumental stone portal of the Cathedral in Trogir made by the master Radovan in 1240. These are masterpieces of European sculpture.

The Gothic period of the Renaissance in the fifteenth century was characterized by the works of the famous sculptor and builder Juraj Matejev called »Dalmatinac«. He built the Cathedral of St. Jacob with the baptismal font, the portraits of his contemporaries, the famous altar of St. Staša in the Cathedral in Split, the magnificent Minčeta tower in Dubrovnik and many other buildings. From the end of the fourteenth to the first decades of the sixteenth century, »the Dalmatian school of painting« was flourishing, represented by the Gothic painters Blaž Jurjev of Trogir, Nikola Vladanov of Šibenik, Dujam Vušković from Split and Lovro Dobričević and his son Vicko from Kotor. In the second half of the fifteenth century, the walls of the Istrian churches were painted by the remarkable Gothic painter Vincent from Kastav such as »Dance of Death« in the church of St. Mary in Škrilinah near Berm, »the Adoration of the Magi«

⇦ *Main city square – the heart of Split*

Magnificent amphitheatre, the popular Arena from the 1st C A.D. in Pula

The Triumphal Arch to Sergijevci, 1st C A.D

Vid – archaeological riches of the ancient town of Narona

Poreč, Basilica of Euphrasius, 6th C A.D., an ⇨ exceptional building of the Byzantine art

Luxurious mosaics in the apse of the Euphrasiana in Poreč

Euphrasiana, Poreč, the mosaic of fish, an early Christian symbol of Christ

Magnificent interior of the Basilica of Euphrasius in Poreč ⇨

The Basilica of Euphrasius in Poreč, remains of a mosaic

Punat, island of Krk, the early Romanesque church of St Dunat

Ruins of the early Croatian church of St Saviour at the source of the Cetina River

Monumental early medieval rotunda of St Donat in Zadar

Rab, interior of the Romanesque church of St Mary the Great

Interior of the cathedral of Mary's Assumption at Osor, an ancient town on the island of Cres

Four stone bell-towers, symbols of ⇨ the town of Rab

Zadar, silver chest of St Šimun, a precious work of art of Croatian goldsmith's trade, 1380

Gold and silver of Zadar and Nin, a small cross, reliquary, 8th C A.D.

Gold and silver of Zadar and Nin, reliquary of St Jacob's head, 11th C

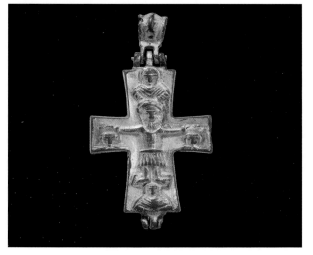

⇦ *Zadar, three-aisled Romanesque cathedral of St Stošija*

Gold and silver of Zadar and Nin, reliquary of St Krševan, 1326

*Gold and silver of Zadar and Nin, Paolo
Veneziano, Our Lady, 14th C*

Zadar building pearls – church of St Mary, convent of Benedictine nuns and a massive Romanesque bell-tower

Zadar, Our Lady with the Child, the work of a local painter, 15th C

St Stošija on the altar of St Martin in the Zadar cathedral, the work of V. Carpaccio, Gold and Silver of Zadar and Nin

Apses of the Romanesque church of St Krševan in Zadar, they are the most beautiful objects in the church

Ugljan polyptych, Ivan Petrov from Milan, 15th C, the Art Collection of the Zadar Franciscans

Detail of the Šibenik cathedral, a harmony of stone

*Frieze of human heads on the Šibenik cathedral,
a magnificent work of Master Juraj Dalmatinac*

⇦ *Famous cathedral of St Jacob in Šibenik and
a monument to Master Juraj Dalmatinac*

Lion gate of the Šibenik cathedral with figures of Adam and Eve supported by lions, a masterpiece of Juraj Dalmatinac

The baptistery in the Šibenik cathedral a unique ⇨ artefact of Croatian and European architecture

High altar in the Šibenik cathedral

Impressive interior of the three-aisled Šibenik cathedral

Trogir cathedral of St Lawrence was built at the beginning of the 13th C in the Romanesque style

Trogir cathedral, portal by Master Radovan and the entrance to the baptistery

in Butoniga, St. John's church and the paintings in the church of St. Trinity in Hrastovlje. The church of St. Roco in Draguć was hand-painted by the local master Anton.

The Gothic period was characterized by masterpieces of medieval goldsmith's artistry such as the box of St. Simeon in Zadar (about 1380) made by Franjo from Milan. The initials and miniatures of the well-known glagolithic missals of Duke Novak Disislavić (1368) and Duke Hrvoje Vukčić Hrvatinić (beginning of the fifteenth century) are also precious.

In the Renaissance period, the most famous Croatian painters were Nikola Božidarević from Dubrovnik (about 1460-1517) and Mihajlo Hamzić (died in 1518). The world -renowed miniaturist Julije Klović Croata (1498-1578) from Grižan in Vinodol was active in Italy and at the court in Budim where he was the head of the court's workshop of miniaturists where Feliks Petančić (1455-1517) from Dubrovnik participated as well.

The construction of the Cathedral in Šibenik built in the Renaissance style was completed by Nikola Firentinac (Nicholas from Florence) (died

*Crucifixion, Blaž
Jurjev Trogiranin,
around 1440, in
Trogir cathedral*

in 1505). In collaboration with Andrija Aleši
(about 1420-1505) and Ivan Dukanović (1440-
1509), he constructed the chapel of the blessed
John in the Cathedral in Trogir. A skillful Renaissance sculptor was Franjo Vranjanin (about 1420-
1502). Dubrovnik as a pearl of European architecture flourished during the Gothic period and the
Renaissance period during the fifteenth and the
sixteenth century.

The Ottoman conquests and their permanent invasions demanded the construction of walled towns
such as Karlovac (1579) which is a typical example
of Renaissance town planning, fortified in the shape
of a sixpointed star, then followed Veliki Tabor in
Hrvatsko Zagorje, the fort in Sisak, the fort of Klis
near Split was built in a Gothic and Renaissance
style, the fortified summer residence called »Tvrdalj« of Petar Hektorović in Stari Grad on the island of Hvar etc.

Interior of the tree-aisled Trogir cathedral

71

Radovan's portal, 1240, Cathedral of St Lawrence

Town of Hvar, Renaissance cathedral of St Stephen

Town of Hvar with its medieval walls and forts

Fish pond at Tvrdalj, the castle of Petar Hektorović in Stari Grad, 16th C

Franciscan Monastery in Hvar, "Last Supper", Matteo Ponzoni-Pončun, 17th C

Dominican Monastery in Stari Grad, Jacopo Tintoretto, "Laying Down into the Tomb", 16th C

Vrboska, the church-fort of St Mary, 16th C

Blaca on the south side of the island of Brač, previous Glagolitic desert

Dominican Monastery of Our Lady of Grace at Glavica in Bol

*Jacopo and Domenico Tintoretto,
painting on the high altar of the
Dominican church in Bol*

*The bell-tower of the cathedral of St Mark ⇨
rises above burning Korčula roofs*

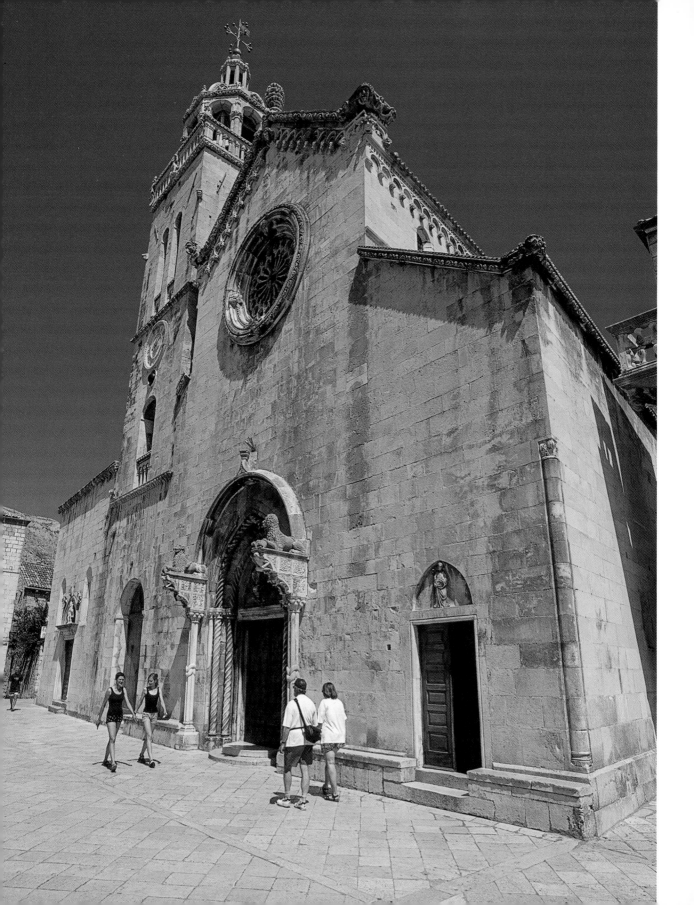

Main aisle of the Korčula cathedral and the ciborium of Marko Andrijić from 1486

⇦ *Harmonious façade of the Gothic-Renaissance Korčula cathedral*

"Annunciation", school of Jacopo Tintoretto, 16th C in the Korčula cathedral

Korčula, the brotherhood of All Saints, a collection of Byzantine icons

Korčula, Abbatial Treasury of St Mark, polyptych of Our Lady, Blaž Jurjev Trogiranin, 15th C

Korčula, the church of All Saints, high altar

Church of All Saints in Korčula,
polyptych of All Saints, Blaž Jurjev
Trogiranin, 15th C

Monastery and Romanesque church of St Mary on the islet of St Mary amidst the Large Lake on the island of Mljet

⇦ *Ancient Ston with salt works from the time of the Republic of Dubrovnik and its round defence walls connecting it with Mali Ston*

Medieval Dubrovnik walls and the round Minčeta Tower

Cloisters of the Franciscan Monastery of Minor Brothers in Dubrovnik

Well in the cloisters of the Dominican Monastery in Dubrovnik

Stradun – the main Dubrovnik street

*Dubrovnik, Large Onofrio's Fountain
from the 15th C*

*One of the entrances to the Franciscan church of
Minor Brothers in Dubrovnik*

Spacious interior of the Dubrovnik Franciscan church

Dubrovnik, old town

Museum of the Dominican Monastery in Dubrovnik, a detail of the triptych, the work of Nikola Božidarević, 16th C

Museum of the Dominican Monastery in Dubrovnik, a triptych, the work of Mihajlo Hamzić, 1512

Museum of the Dominican Monastery in Dubrovnik, polyptych Christ's Baptism, the work of Lovro Dobričević from 1448

The Jesuits brought Baroque architecture to Croatia. They built the church of St. Catherine in Zagreb (between 1620 and 1631) and the church of the Annunciation of the Virgin Mary in Varaždin. In northern Croatia, Baroque was a predominant style in architecture.

The coastal part of Croatia was not so much under the influence of the Baroque style except for the grand rotunda of the church of St. Vid in Rijeka, St. Mary's Cathedral and the Jesuit's church of St. Blaise in Dubrovnik.

The prominent Baroque painters were Bernardo Bobić (1683) who painted the altar paintings at the church of St. Catherine in Zagreb, Tripo Kokolja

(1661-1713) from Perast in Boka Kotorska and the Paulist painter Ivan Ranger (1700-1753) who painted the churches in Belec, Purga, Štrigova and Lepoglava and Federico Benković (1677-1753) who painted abroad. His painting »The Abraham's Victim« is exhibited in the Strossmayer's gallery of old masters in the Croatian Academy of Arts and Sciences in Zagreb. During the nineteenth century, in the period of the so-called »neostyles« and »historical styles«, Zagreb was a leading town in the politics and culture of the Croats with characteristics of a modern European capital. Besides Zagreb, many public buildings, churches, palaces, theatres, castles and gardens were designed and

Motovun, a small mediaval town with the preserved old town ⇨

"Dance Macabre", a detail from the fresco by Vincent from Kastav in the church of St Mary on Škrinilah, 1474, Beram

Rovinj, a famous historical, cultural and tourist centre of Istria

constructed in other Croatian towns such as the neoRomanesque Cathedral in Đakovo, theatres in Rijeka and Osijek, the Governor's Palace in Rijeka, the Prokurative in Split etc.

Enormous contributions to the development of economics, the foundation of new public institutions and the construction of a number of buildings such as the hospital, the Academy, the galleries and the libraries (the Croatian University, the Cathedral in Đakovo, the gardens etc.) are at-

Rovinj, the baptistery of the Holy Trinity from the 13th C, a pearl of Romanesque architecture

⇦ *Oprtalj, the church of St Mary with the frescoes of Master Klerigin from Koper, 15th C*

Karlovac, a masterpiece of the Renaissance town-planning art

Karlovac, a detail of the town

Karlovac, a town of pearls

*Towers of the Zagreb cathedral and the bell-tower of the church ⇨
of St Mary at Dolac*

97

The Treasury of the Zagreb Cathedral

Monstrance, Hans Georg Pfisterer, Graz, 1738

A detail from Ladislav's mantle, 11th C

Bishop Osvald Thuz's pastoral, 15th C

Ivory diptych, 11th C, a metal frame, 17th C

Missal of Juraj from Topusko, Zagreb, Budim, 15/16th C

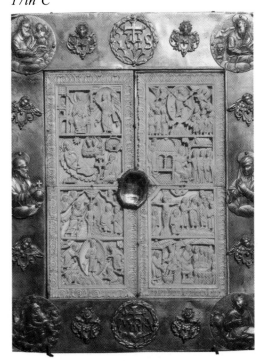

⇦ Interior of the neo-Gothic Zagreb cathedral of St Stephen

Church of St Mark on the main square in ⇨ the Upper Town, Zagreb

Church of St Katherine, the most beautiful Zagreb sacred building

Interior of the church of St Katherine is adorned with stucco decorations

Kamenita vrata (Stone Gate), in front of the miraculous painting of Our Lady, Zagreb

Impressive arcades on the central Zagreb city cemetery Mirogoj

Trakošćan Castle rises on a hill above the lake surrounded by beautiful pleasure gardens

⇦ *Samobor, a picturesque small town in the immediate vicinity of Zagreb*

Veliki Tabor, a fort-castle, a precious memento to the fortifications art of building

Interior of the Baroque Paulinist church in Lepoglava

Belec, a detail of luxurious interior of the church of Our Lady of the Snows

High altar of Our Lady of the Snows in Kutina, a unique Baroque composition

⇦ *Interior of the church of Our Lady of the Snows, an exceptional work of Croatian Baroque*

Gilt interior of the Varaždin cathedral of the Assumption of Our Lady, a high Baroque phase

Fortified old town of Varaždin, a preserved example of fortifications building

Čakovec, the old and new castle within medieval walls

Čakovec, the central town square

Marija Bistrica, the best known Mary shrine and place of pilgrimage

tributed to two archibishops and maecenas of the Croatian culture, i.e. to Maximilian Vrhovec, the Archbishop of Zagreb (1752-1827) and to Josip Juraj Strossmayer, the Archbishop of Đakovo (1815-1905).

Modern Croatian architecture developed at the beginning of the twentieth century and the architect Victor Kovačić (1874-1924) is considered its spiritual father. He was responsible for the palace of the Burse and the church of St. Blaise in Zagreb with its large reinforced concrete dome, one of the first such structures in the world.

The painter Vjekoslav Karas (1821-1858) from Karlovac, the sculptors Ivan Rendić (1849-1932) from Imotski, Robert Valdec (1872-1929) from Krapina and Robert Frangeš-Mihanović (1872-1940) born in Srijemska Mitrovica, also belong to this period.

Large paintings representing events from Croatian history such as the arrival and christening of the Croat kings Tomislav, Zrinski and Frankopan were painted in the nineteenth century by Ferdo Quiquerez (1845-1893), Oton Iveković (1869-1939), Mato Celestin Medović (1857-1920) and Bela Čikoš-Sesija (1864-1931). Vlaho Bukovac (1855-1923) was a prominent painter in the Zagreb art circle at the beginning of the twentieth century. He was born in Cavtat and he painted such masterpieces as »Gundulić's Dream« and the »Croatian Revival« which is painted on the gala

Požega, a cultural and historical centre of the picturesque Požega basin

Kutjevo Castle

New Pejačević Castle with the Franciscan Monastery and the church of St Anthony in Našice

Donji Miholjac, a castle with spacious park area

Interior of the neor-Romanesque three-aisled cathedral of St Peter in Đakovo

curtain of the Croatian national theatre in Zagreb. Slava Raškaj (1877-1906) was especially successful with water colours.

The post-impressionists Emanuel Vidović (1870-1953), Josip Račić (1885-1908), Miroslav Kraljević (1885-1913) and Vladimir Becić (1886-1954) painted their impressions from nature. Social situations and rural life were painted by the painters belonging to the »Zemlja« (Earth) artistic group. Krsto Hegedušić (1901-1975) was its prominent representative. He established the world famous school of naiive paintings in Hlebine. The main representatives of the same school are Ivan Generalić (1914-1992), Mirko Virius (1889-1943), Ivan Lacković Croata (born in 1932), Mijo Kovačić (born in 1935) and the world reputed Ivan Rabuzin (born in 1921).

The period of the Croatian paintings after World War II was characterized by the surrealist Miljenko Stančić (1926-1977), Edo Murtić (born in 1921), the painter of abstract paintings and Ivo Dulčić (1916-1975) the painter of religious scenes. Oton Gliha (born in 1914) and Frano Šimunović (1908-1995) achieved a particular artistic expression.

The works of the sculptor Ivan Meštrović (1883-1962), are »The History of the Croats«, »The Well of Life«, the sculputure of J.J. Strossmayer in Zagreb and those of Grgur Ninski in Split, the mausoleum of the Račić family in Cavtat and one dedicated to his family in Otavice near Drniš. His student Antun Augustinčić (1900-1979) made a sculpture named »Peace« which is located in front of the UN building in New York. Meštrović, Augustinčić and F. Kršinić (1897-1982) formed the so-called triumvirate of modern Croatian sculpture. Beside these sculptors, there are also many others whose works are worth admiring.

Đakovo Cathedral, "the honourable crown of beautiful Slavonia" ⇨

Osijek, interior of the parish church of Sts Peter and Paul

⇦ *Magnificent neo-Gothic three-aisled church of Sts Peter and Paul in Osijek*

Ilok, the monastery and church of St John Capistrano and the Odescalchi Castle ⇨

Shooting Castle at Bilje from the 18th C

Eltz Castle and Town Museum of Vukovar

"Fountain of Life" by Ivan Meštrović, an exceptional artistic achievement

LITERATURE

*T*he most ancient records were carved in stone during the Greek colonization of the Dalmatian islands in the fourth century B.C. With the arrival of the Romans the Latin language became the predominant language in public official communication and in the private sphere, and thus became the universal form of written communication.

During their history, the Croats were using three different languages, i.e. Latin (up to the first half of the nineteenth century), Old Slavic (from the ninth to the twentieth century) or the Croatian and Slavic type used in the church liturgy (from the twelfth to the sixteenth century) and the Croatian literary language (at first, the chakavian dialect) as written on the Plate from Baška in 1100. They were also using three alphabets, i.e. Latin, the Croatian Latin derived from the Glagolitic and the Cyrillic one (the Croatian variant). The first centers of Croatian literacy were situated along the coast. When the diocese of Zagreb was founded in 1094, new centers were spreading rapidly in the hinterland. In the thirteenth century, the centre of literacy in medieval Slavonia was the church in Čazma. The Croats were among the first in Europe to have their own printed book, the so-called Glagolitic missal from 1483.

Povaljska listina (Povlja Charter), one of the oldest Croatian documents written in Cyrillic script, 1250 (island of Brač)

Senj Glagolitic missal from 1494

"Baščanska ploča" (Baška Tablet) from the church of St Lucy at Jurandvor near Baška on the island of Krk, the oldest document in the Croatian language, 11th C

The first documents which mention the names of the Croatian dukes Trpimir, Branimir, Muncimir and other dignitaries were carved in Latin and they date as early as the eleventh century. Monuments carved in the Glagolitic alphabet are the inscriptions from Plomin and Krk dating from the eleventh and twelfth century, the Plate from Valun written in Latin and the Plate from Senj. Legal documents written in the Glagolitic and the Croatian scripts are represented in the Code of Vinodol from 1288 and the Istrian divorce record from the thirteenth century.

Croatian texts written in the Cyrillic alphabet are Povljanski prag from 1184 and the List from Povlja from 1250 whose original dates from 1184 (the island of Brač). The Code from Poljice (before 1440) was also written in the Croatian and Cyrillic alphabets.

Croatian texts written in Latin date from the fourteenth century on, (such as the Code of Zadar from 1345 and the Prayer of Šibenik from 1347). The Croatian writers of Latin texts were part of the European group of Latin writers. Marko Marulić (was one among them whose works

Monument to Marko Marulić, a poet and thinker, "the father of Croatian literature" in Split

Monument to the poet f. Andrija Kačić Miošić in Makarska

were translated into major European languages and Ivan Česmički /Ianus Pannonius/ (1434-1472). Many Latin writers were also writing in Croatian, thus Marko Marulić is considered the »father« of Croatian literature with his work entitled »Judita«.

The writers of the medieval and more recent Croatian literature were Hanibal Lucić (1485-1553), Petar Hektorović (1487-1572), Petar Zoranić (1508-?), Marin Držić (1508-1567), Ivan Gundulić (1589-1638), Ivan Bunić Vučić (1591-1658), Junije Palmotić (1607-1657), Pavao Ritter Vitezović (1621-1671), Andrija Kačić Miošić (1704-1760),

Tituš Brezovački (1757-1805), Ivan Mažuranić (1814-1891), August Šenoa (1838-1881), Eugen Kumičić (1850-1904), Ante Kovačić (1854-1889), Ksaver Šandor Gjalski (18541935), Silvije Strahimir Kranjčević (1865-1908), Antun Gustav Matoš (1873-1914), Ivana Brlić-Mažuranić (1874-1938), Vladimir Nazor (1876-1949), Tin Ujević (1891-1955), Mile Budak (1889-1945), August Cesarec (1893-1941), Miroslav Krleža (1893-1981), Dobriša Cesarić (1902-1980), Dragutin Tadijanović (1905), Ivan Goran Kovačić (1913-1943), Ranko Marinković (1913), Ivan Raos (1921-1987), Josip Pupačić (1928-1971) etc.

SCIENCE AND EDUCATION

The work of a number of Croatian scientists has contributed to the achievements of world science. Herman Dalmatin (12th c.) with his excellent knowledge of astronomy, mathematics and natural philosophy had a prominent position among the European scientists of his time, whilst the texts describing his journeys along with his translations contributed to a better understanding of Eastern and Arabian cultures. The merchant from Dubrovnik Benko Kotruljević (died around 1468) was a philosopher and a physicist but he also wrote about book-keeping, Nikola Gučetić (1549-1610), the mathematician Marin Getaldić (1566-1626), Pavo Skalić (1534-1575), the encyclopaedist from Zagreb, the remarkable scientist and philosopher Franjo Petrić (1529-1597), a skillfull language expert and the writer of the first Croatian grammar Bartol Kašić (1575-1650), a historian, lexicographer and an inventor Faust Vrančić from Šibenik (1551-1617), the editor of a dictionary written in five languages (Latin-Italian German-Croatian-Hungarian) who in his work *Machinae novae* (1595) anticipated a great number of technical inventions such as the oldest known parachute. Among the most innovative scientists was Ruđer Bošković (1711-1787), a physicist, mathematician, astronomer, philosopher, surveyor, technician and a diplomat. In the field of science, there was seismologist Andro Mohorovičić (1857-1936) and a genius in the field of electrical engineering Nikola Tesla (1856-1943). The founder of the dactyloscopy, the identification of finger prints, was Ivan Vučetić, the inventor of the first mechanical pen was Slavoljub Penkala (1871-1922) and there was the Nobel Prize winners chemists Lavoslav Ružička (1887-1976) and

Vladimir Prelog (1906-1998). The development of the educational system in Croatia began from the ninth century on when the Benedictines were active on the courts of Croatian dukes. The first public schools were opened in the tweltfth century, in Zadar (1282), in Dubrovnik (1333) and in Zagreb (1362). According to recent investigations, the first institution of higher education, i.e. the University was founded in 1396 in Zadar which in 1553 received a status of a »privileged University«.

Present-day universities in Zagreb, Split, Osijek and Rijeka, along with professional schools and high schools which the students attend after compulsory primary education, are the basis for the education of Croatia's scientists.

The highest ranking scientific institution is the Croatian Academy of Arts and Sciences (HAZU) which was founded in 1861 as the Yugoslav Academy of Arts and Sciences (JAZU), the first institution of its kind in »the South inhabited by the Slavs«. The king confirmed its foundation in 1863.

Man of Vukovar, Lavoslav Ružička, the Nobel ⇨
Prize winner for chemistry in 1939

Palace of the Croatian Academy of Sciences and Arts in Zagreb

Senate House of the University of Zagreb with Meštrović's sculpture "History of the Croats"

National and University Library in Zagreb

THEATRE, A SPIRIT OF INNOVATION AND CREATIVE FILM ART

*T*he remains of the Roman theatres in Salona near Split, in Pula and on the island of Vis reveal a rich theatre life in ancient times. The presence of the actors in ancient Siscia (Sisak) is confirmed by an inscription on the grave of a leader of the group of actors which says:

»I was dead many times (on stage) but never like this time«. The findings also confirm theatrical activities during the Medieval Times in Dubrovnik, Split, Hvar, Zagreb, Vukovar and in other towns. The first known theatre house, one of the oldest in Europe, was built in 1612 on the island of Hvar which is still in use today. During the nineteenth century, the theatre houses in Zagreb, Pula, Rijeka, Zadar, Šibenik, Split, Dubrovnik, Varaždin, Karlovac and Osijek were built.

Nowdays, the centre of Croatian theatrical life is Zagreb where besides the Croatian National Theatre with its three departments of drama, opera and ballet, there are also several other theatres like the Gavella theatre of drama, the Comedy

Theatre in the town of Hvar – one of the oldest in Europe, built in 1612

Neo-Baroque building of the Croatian People's Theatre in Zagreb

Curtain of the Croatian People's Theatre in Zagreb depicting the Croatian National Revival, a splendid work of Vlaho Bukovac

theatre, the ITD theatre, the Zagreb Youth Theatre, the Kerempuh theatre of satire etc. There are theatres also in Split, Osijek, Virovitica, Varaždin, Dubrovnik, Karlovac and Rijeka (where the Italian drama is active among the Italian minority group). There are also puppet-shows in Rijeka, Zadar, Split, Osijek and in Zagreb. There are several youth theatres, independent groups of actors and non-professional groups of actors.

During the year, different theatre festivals take place throughout Croatia. There is a long tradition of the Gavella Nights, the Days of satire in Zagreb

Split Summer, the performance of Aida at Peristil

Osijek, the exceptional building of the Croatian National Theatre

The building of the Croatian National Theatre in Split

The solemn opening of the Dubrovnik Summer Festival

and the Eurokaz, the international festival of a new theatre. The more recent ones are the Marulić Days in Split, the Croatian festival of small scenes in Rijeka, the festival of actors in Vinkovci, the Krleža's Days in Osijek whilst the amateurs have their own festivals which take place on a regular and voluntary basis. The summer festival in Dubrovnik and the Split Summer Festival with their splendid drama performances enrich cultural life during the summer season. The festival of puppet-shows in Zagreb and the children's festival in Šibenik are of international importance.

FILM

Zagreb already had its first film performance in 1896 only a year after the Paris performance. Since 1907 there are permanent cinemas in Zagreb and in 1917 the Croatia Film was founded. A festival of Croatian films is held each year in the Arena in Pula, aswell as the Days of Croatian Film festival in Zagreb and at the Motovun Film Festival.

Croatian documentaries and cartoons have had significant success at international film festivals. The first cartoon made in Zagreb was in 1922 and the Cartoon studio was founded in 1956. The unique achievements of their authors from »the Zagreb school of cartoons« are highly regarded by the critics with about 150 awards received at international festivals and the Oscar prize awarded in 1962 for the nomination of the »Surogate« by Dušan Vukotić. The cartoons like »Professor Baltazar« and »The Flying Bears« cheer up children all over the world. Due to the world reputation of its cartoon creators, Zagreb hosted the Biannual world festival of animated films in 1972 which is one among four of the most reputed film festivals in the world.

MUSIC AND MUSICAL PERFORMANCES

Written documents testify that the tradition of artistic music in Croatia is at least ten centuries old. The first modern opera »Love and Malice« (1846) and »Porin« (1851) by Vatroslav Lisinski (1819-1854) confirmed the works of Ivan Zajc (1832-1914) the author of the famous patriotic opera »Nikola Šubić Zrinski« and Crotia's musical creativity by performing in the local language. The tradition was continued with the twentieth century composers Antun Dobrinić (1878-1955), Ivan Matetić-Ronjgov (1880-1960), Josip Stolcer Slavenski (1896-1955), Jakov Gotovac (1895-1982) with his comic opera »Ero from the Other World«, Ivo Tijardović (1895-1976) with his popular operettas the »Little Floramye« and the »Split's Aquarelle«, the ballet composers Fran Lothka (1883-1962) with his »Devil in the Village« and Krešimir Baranović (1894-1975) with »A Fancy Heart«.

Numerous Croatian musicians of the twentieth century are world renowed such as the violinists Zlatko Baloković (1895-1965) and Stjepan Šulek (1914-1986), the opera singers, the barytones Josip Kašman (1880-1925) who was singing in the first season at the Metropolitan Opera House and Vladimir Ruždjak (1922-1987), the sopranos Milka Trnina (1863-1941) and her student, the primadona of the Metropolitan Opera House Zinka Kunc (1906-1989), the queen of the Viennese Opera House, the soprano Srebrenka Jurinac (1921), the mezzosoprano Ruža Pospiš-Baldani, the conductors Lovro Matačić (1899-1985), Berislav Klobučar (1924) and Vjekoslav Šutej (1951) and the virtuoso pianist Ivo Pogorelić (1958) etc. Among vocalists, the Zagreb Solists and the Philpharmonic orchestra have garnered international fame and recognition.

The musical performances are as follows: the Zagreb Musical Biannual, the Summer Festival in Dubrovnik, the Split Summer Festival (opera and concert performances), summer performances on the island of Krk, Musical evenings at St. Donat

Concert of classical music in the atrium of the Rector's Palace in Dubrovnik

in Zadar dedicated to old music, the Varaždin Baroque Evenings, the Osor Musical Evenings, the Zagreb Summer Festival of Symphonic, Chamber, Popular and Organist Music, the Summer festival of opera and ballet in Opatija, opera performances in the Arena in Pula etc. Concerts of classical music take place during the summer season on the islands of Vis, Hvar, and Rab as well as in Poreč and Rovinj. The memorials »Josip Slavenski« in Čakovec, »Darko Lukić« and »Franjo Krežma« in Osijek and »Dora Pejačević« in Našice are also worth mentioning. Among the festivals of local and traditional singing, the most famous are the July festival featuring groups of Dalmatian singers in the atmospheric old town of Omiš, the Festi-

val of the Kajkavian Songs in Krapina, the festival of the singing groups in Klis and a number of festivals of local importance.

Croatian popular music (pop, rock etc.) is rich both in solists and in vocal and instrumental groups, and is performed all year round throughout Croatia. Festivals of popular music are especially valued like the Zagreb-fest, the Split festival and the Melodies of the Croatian Adriatic in Split, the Zadarfest, the festival in Opatija and the Melodies of Istria and the Kvarner. There are two big events on the Croatian musical scene - Dora, the competition of Croatian songs for the Eurovision Song Contest and Porin, an award for the best Croatian discographic achievement.

SPORTS AND RECREATION

*T*he Croats live for sport, sport culture and fair play. There is no country in the world, with such a comparatively small number of inhabitants and so many top sportsmen and women in different sporting disciplines (basket ball, hand ball, waterpolo, swimming, tennis, table tennis, boxing and fighting sports, football, rowing etc.). The Croatian hand-ball players won the gold medal at the Olympic games in 1996 in Atlanta which was the first gold medal won after the recognition of Croatia as an independent state.

With their knowledge and efficiency, a great number of Croatian sportsmen and coaches are highly acclaimed all over the world. Among them are the legends of the Croatian and world basketball, the late Krešimir Ćosić from Zadar and tragically deceased Dražen Petrović from Šibenik whose sport, human and patriotic virtues Croatia will always remember.

The museum of famous sportsmen in the USA bears the name of Krešimir Ćosić among the names of the world's best basketball players, whilst the Olympic board erected a monument in honour to Dražen Petrović in Lausanne, Switzerland.

Large sporting contests such as the Mediterranean Games in 1979, the 1990 European Championship in athletics in Split and the World University Games in Zagreb in 1987 have been successfully organized in Croatia.

Janica Kostelić, "the snow queen" and one of the best world skiers, the most successful skier of all times by the number of the acquired golden medals in the Olympic Games

Croatian tennis players, the winners of the Davis Cup

Croatian "golden" handball players

Football players in the recognisable dresses of the Croatian team

MUSEUMS, BEARING WITNESSES TO SURVIVAL

The cultural and historical heritage of the Croatian people has been exhibited in numerous museums, libraries, archives and other cultural and scientific institutions. The Croatian state archives were founded in 1643 in Zagreb (the records are 25 km long). Other archives include the National and University Library (founded in 1606 with almost 2.5 millions of books), the Metropolitan library with rare and precious books (liturgical books from the times when the diocese in Zagreb was founded in 1094), the Science Museum with three separate collections (zoological, geological and paleontological and mineralogical and petrographic), the Historical Museum, the Archeological Museum (with its Egyptian and coin collection, a collection from Prehistoric and the Ancient times including the longest Etruscian text in the world (15 m long)

Hušnjakovo brdo, the prehistoric man of Krapina (homo primigenius krapiensis)

Museum of Croatian Archaeological Monuments in Split

Zagreb, the neo-Renaissance building of the Mimara Museum

Metković, Ornithological Collection

and a collection from the Middle Ages), the Museum for Arts and Crafts, the Ethnographic Museum, the Technical Museum, the Hunting Museum, the Meštrović Museum, the Mimara Museum and many others. There are also quite a number of galleries like the Strossmayer's gallery of old masters, the Modern gallery, the Gallery of modern art, etc.

The first archeological museum was founded in 1820 in Split where the more recent Museum of Croatian Archeological Monuments is also situated. Archeological museums are also situated in Pula and Zadar whilst almost every Croatian town has its own town museum with archeological, historical, ethnographic and artistic data. Data on the history of Croats and their relationship with the sea can be seen in the maritime museums in Rijeka, Split, Orebić and Dubrovnik. A museum on fish is situated in Vrboska, on the island of Hvar and there are also other different collections here. The secrets and wonders of the submarine life can be seen at aquariums in Dubrovnik and Rovinj and in the Malacological museum of the Franciscan monastery in Makarska. There is a museum on the evolution of man situated in Krapina and one on the peasants' rebellion in Gornja Stubica. There are different memorial museums celebrating famous Croatian artists and scientists in their birth places such as the museum in memomory of I.G. Kovačić in Lukovdol, Nikola Tesla in Smiljan, I. Meštrović in Split and Zagreb, V. Bukovac in Cavtat and P. Preradović in Grabrovnica in Podravina. These are all worth visiting. The cathedrals in Zagreb and Split and the churches and monasteris along the Croatian coast house a rich collection of valuable books and works of art.

The diversity and richness of plant life can be admired in the botanical gardens in Zagreb, in the Velebit botanical garden in Modriča doc, the school botanical garden of the Educational Academy in Split (on the Marjan hill), the Biokovo botanical garden in Kotišina and the arboretums in Trsteno and Opeka (near Vinica, not far from Varaždin). Bird lovers can visit the unique Ruener ornitological collection in Metković or the Zoological museum of Baranja in Kopačevo.

FOLKLORE HERITAGE

*T*he diversity and the beauty of the landscape, its environment, customs and the way of life of the people inhabited in Croatia are reflected in the colorful national costumes of Šestine, Bizovac, Đakovo, Imotski and Sinj, Makarska, Konavle, Istria and the islands of Krk, Cres, Susak, Pag etc. The picturesque Croatian folkloric costumes can, according to their characteristics, be divided into the Pannonian, the Dinara and the Adriatic areas.

The interesting fact is, that a tie, which is worn all over the world as a man's apparel, developed from the scarf the Croatian soldiers used to wear. Its name cravate (a tie) derived from the French word »cravate« associated with the members of the Croatian cavalry (the Royal cravat) who were in the service of King Louis XIV (1643-1715).

The displays of various folklore groups play an important role in keeping the folklore traditions alive. The International Festival of Folklore takes place every summer in Zagreb. There are also other interesting folklore festivals that celebrate the embroidery from Đakovo, the Autumn in Vinkovci, the Youth and Beauty of Slavonia in Stari Mikanovci and the Contest for the most attractive girl in Slavonia.

Attractive International Review of Folklore in Zagreb

Luxurious headgear of the Slavonian folk costume

Various fish feasts, the election of local »kings«, the carnivals which take place both on the coast and in the hinterland, like the one in Samobor, the dances from the islands of Susak and Pag, the »tanec« dance from the island of Krk and the linđo from Dubrovnik contribute to the richness of Croatia's national customs. Special tourist attractions are the knights' dances called the »moreška« from Korčula and the »kumpanija« or the »mostra« from Blato. The famous feast of »The iron-ring from Sinj« is held in August as a reminder of the victory of the people of Sinj over the Ottomans in 1715. On this occasion the horsemen dressed in historical costumes and ride a horse and try to hit the center of the ring. The same game is played in

Traditional folklore performance in Županja, variety of folk costumes and the parade of Lippizaner horses

Carnival festivities – bell-ringers chase away winter and call spring

Female folk costume of the island Pag with its famous lace on the head scarf

Solemn female folk costume of the island of Susak, fluttering and full of colours

Barban in Istria. The traditional »Competition of old Sports« in Brodanac show the tradition and customs of the local people.

Celebrations for Christmas and Easter, the tradition of which has never ceased show the reverence of the Croats for the Catholic faith and for the preservation of their ancestral customs.

Picturesque folk costume of Vrlika – girls dancing in rapture

Alka player in his solemn costume preparing for the chivalrous competition in the "Sinjska alka"

Luxurious male and female folk costumes of Konavle

Korčula, traditional chivalrous play "Moreška" accompanied with the sword dance

RICHNESS OF CROATIAN TABLE

*B*esides the traditional European cuisine, Croatian restaurants offer a variety of local dishes. Among the appetizers, there is Dalmatian smoked ham, the Gavrilović salami, sausages from Istria and Slavonia, salted sardines, sheep's cheese from Pag and other delicacies. Fish is prepared in different ways and especially tasty are the »brodet« made of sea fish, the fresh-water fish stew and the Neretva brodet made of eels and frogs. Among the meat dishes, there is the Dalmatian pasticada (a steak), the Zagreb veal cutlet, the Zagorje cutlet, breaded veal slices, roasted turkey with a kind of pastry, black pudding with hard-boiled corn mush and sauerkraut, roasted lamb meat prepared in a special oven,

etc. In northern Croatia, the venison is always prepared in a creamy sauce, whilst in Dalmatia it is prepared in a sauce made of olive oil, vineger, wine, a sweet kind of wine, prunes, lemon juice and a touch of rosemary and other aromatic herbs.

Local types of brandy are also appreciated such as herbal brandy, grape brandy, plum brandy, walnut brandy, Istrian brandy, etc.

»Croatia is a an aboundant country
oh, Lord bless our vine,
Its clear drop is more valuable than
gold itself,
It is praised all over the world!«

(A. Šenoa)

Traditional Croatian cuisine provides a rich choice of various specialities

A glass of good wine goes along with a delicious dish and Croatia is renowed for the variety of its wine. In the ancient times (third or second century B.C.) a Greek writer from the area of Croatia had said: »*On the island of Vis there is such a fine wine in comparaison with other sorts of wine*«

Croatia with its 70,000 hectares of vinyards is on the 25th place in the world and on the 12th place in Europe. The natural conditions such as relief, soil, climate and the type of grape determine the production of the wine and its origin.

The regions of grape-growing are divided into the continental and coastal, with different types of grapes suitable for the production of fine red and white wines depending on geographical provenance. The most famous types of grapes are plavac (central and southern Dalmatia with its islands), suitable for the production of excellent Croatian wine varieties such as Plavac, Dingač, Postup, Faros etc.

Other parts of Croatia are known for the following varieties of wine: Malvazija and Pinot from Istria, Žlahtina from the island of Krk and Graševina, Riesling and Traminac from Đakovo. The so-called wine roads traversing the area of vinyards with attractive wine-cellars and restaurants situated in the vicinity of Jastrebarsko, Samobor, Donja Zelina, Istria, Moslavina and the road between Popovača and Kutina are worth visiting.

Modern airports have brought Croatia closer to Europe and the world

TRAFFIC CONNECTIONS

Croatia has always been an international crossroad. The so-called Amber Road in prehistoric times was a crossing from the north of Europe to the ports of Eastern Medeterranean. The first solid roads were built by the Romans such as the one leading from Aquillea, through Rijeka to Zadar, Skradin, Solin, Vid (near Metković), Cavtat and further down through Via Egnatia to Drac and Solun. A special road network linked the Adriatic coast with the hinterland (the areas along the Sava and the Danube rivers).

The modern Croatian road network is developing in two longitudinal directions (along the Sava and the Drava rivers and the Adriatic) and the horizontal one (from the Hungarian border, Varaždin, Zagreb, Rijeka and from Maribor via Zagreb to Split. The shortest way from Slavonia to reach the sea is through the Federation of Bosnia and Herzegovina. The development and modernization of the road network in Croatia is a prerequisite for its better connection with the rest of Europe.

An important intercontinental railway line with major roads is passing through Croatia (the Pannonian part), linking Western and Central Europe with South-Eastern Europe and the eastern directions of the railway traffic will follow the road directions.

The exit to the warm Adriatic sea offers Croatia many advantages from the traffic, geographical and economical point of view. There are eight larger ports in Croatia for trans-ocean liners and quite a number of smaller sea ports.

Rijeka is the port with the largest sea traffic, then follow the ports of Ploče, Split and Šibenik. A special port for oil transport is in Omišalj on the island of Krk which is linked by the Adriatic oil pipeline to the interior of the country and further with the Central European countries and the Balkans.

Air traffic is one of the prerequisites for the development of a modern tourist trade in Croatia. The Croatian national air company Croatia Airlines links Croatia with the rest of Europe whilst aircrafts of renowed world air-line companies land at Croatian international airports in Zagreb, Osijek, Pula, Rijeka (on the island of Krk), Zadar, Split and Dubrovnik. There are also some recently constructed smaller airports for small tourist and sport airplanes near Udbina, Sinj and on the islands of Lošinj and Brač while the construction of future airports is planned on the islands of Hvar, Vis, Šolta, Korčula and in the vicinity of other tourist resorts.

Rijeka, a port with the greatest traffic in Croatia

THE ECONOMY

*T*he Croatian economy ranges from agriculture, cattle breeding, fishery, growing of Mediterranean fruits and vegetables, to road and sea traffic, shipbuilding, commerce and tourism. Agriculture is considered the basis of Croatian economic development with 12,000 square kilometers of arable land which is about 57% out of the total area of Croatia. A significant potential is in forests, about 20,000 square kilometers or 36%. Four types of agricultural areas can be distinguished: lowlands, highlands, mountains with valleys and the Adriatic region.

The flat agricultural region is the most important part of Croatia with corn fields and it encircles a larger part of Eastern Croatia and quite a large part of Central Croatia (the central valley, Podravina and Međimurje). Corns like maize and wheat with sugar-beet and oil-seeds are predominant. Pig-breeding is predominant in Turopolje and Slavonia, while cattleraising is most developed in the central valley of the Bjelovar region. Plum and apple-trees grow in Borinci and Kutina. Fishing of carps is also popular.

The hilly region encircles the Pannonian area (being 200 m high) where potatoes are predominant in agriculture. Vinyards are cultivated in the north and in the west while fruit-growing is predominant in the south. Larger pasture areas are suitable for cattle raising.

In the mountains, potatoes, barley, oates, rye and cabbage are cultivated, while plum and apple-trees are predominant in the fruit-growing regions and the herds of sheeps are raised in Lika.

The Adriatic region is known for grapes and fruit growing on little arable land and with some pastures areas on rocky mounts. Grapes and fruits

Cattle breeding has a long tradition

are grown along the coast while wheat and vegetables grow in the interior of the country. Dalmatinska zagora is situated in the hinterland, in the karst area with valleys suitable for the growing of vegetables and rather poor pastures areas for sheep-breeding.

Industry is the main economic activity in Croatia according to the number of people employed in it. In 1991, it contributed about 44% to the national income together with mining and energy resources, the quarter of which refers to Zagreb. Important branches of industry are metal, chemical, food, textile, wood and especially the ship-building industry, being among the largest in the world, based on hundred of years of experience (there are shipyards in Pula, Rijeka, Kraljevica, Mali Lošinj, Trogir, Split, Korčula, Dubrovnik and there are also some smaller dockyards).

Amongst energy resources, oil plays an important role (there are oil sources in Stružec, Žutica, Beničanci, Šandrovac, Đeletovci, natural gas in Lendava). There are also hydro-electric power plants, however the coal mines are mostly closed. The electric power supply is sufficient for about 40% of the total electrical energy consumption, the rest is obtained by means of the thermoelectric power plants (30-40%), and nuclear energy is obtained through the nuclear power plant in Krško (10%) which is jointly owned by Croatia and Slovenia. Electricity is also imported from abroad.

During the Homeland War (1991-1995) Croatia lost many lives and suffered war damages from Serbian aggression which caused huge damage to the economy. Thanks to the country's potential and the fact that Croatia no longer has an obligation to support the former Yugoslav federation, there are good possibilites for global development.

Fishing industry has always been important for the coastal inhabitants

Crucifixion, a moment for rest and praying

142

THE VALUE OF TOURISM

Tourism is a especially important branch of the Croatian economy. Tourism began to develop in parallel with the general European interest in overseas holidays. Austrian and Croatian doctors published in the 1870's a number of books and leaflets on the Croatian coastal resorts, recommending them as health and bathing resorts. Such an atmosphere encouraged the construction of the first hotels in Opatija, Rab, Crikvenica and Lošinj, as well as the establishment of the first tourist associations and the publication of the first tourist guides (1888 in Opatija and Lošinj). After World War I, tourism started to expand and in the thirties there were already about a million tourists on the Adriatic, mainly local people, as well as, Czech, Austrian and German tourists. After World War II, many tourist resorts, hotels, marines and campsites were built and numerous tourist agencies were founded.

In the coastal area, almost 93% of the income is realized through tourism. This includes tourism in the winter season such as the organisation of conferences, health tourism and training for sportspeople. Tourism is also developing in other parts

Opatija, a town of refined beauty, lush vegetation and tourist liveliness

Idyllic islet of Košljun with its Franciscan Monastery holds a valuable artistic heritage, island of Krk

of Croatia which promotes winter holidays and health and recreational trips. The organisation of conferences and health tourism are particularly developed in spas, some of which have existed since the Roman times like the ones in Daruvar (Aquae Balissae), Topusko, Lešće, Istarske toplice (situated between Buzet and Motovun), then follow Lipik, Đakovačka Breznica, Bizovac in Slavonia, Varaždinske toplice (Aquae Jasae), Krapinske toplice (Aqua Vivae), Stubičke toplice, Tuheljske toplice, Sutinske toplice, Šemničke toplice and Novomarofske toplice in the region of Hrvatsko zagorje. Winter tourism is developed in areas suitable for skiing such as the Platak, Bjelolasica and Medvednica mountains.

Croatian tourism includes hunting with 53,000 square kilometers of hunting grounds. The associations of hunters and other specialized institutions ensure accommodation, professional help and offer information to international hunters. Shooting of game and season times are defined by laws

Mali Lošinj, a town of mild climate, long maritime past and rich tourist facilities

Croatia is a well-known sailing destination

Blue Cave on the island of Biševo, one of the most beautiful sea caves in Europe

whilst rare game is protected by the law. Game includes deers, fawns, boars, hares, pheasants, partridges, wild ducks, geese, woodcocks, pigeons, quails, wild black cocks and other animals. Sport fishing on the sea, rivers, lakes and fishponds has also been developed. Sport fishermen should inquire about the law concerning sport fishing. Submarine fishermen and divers can enjoy submarine life but they should also be acquainted with the relevant laws governing the sport. Thousands of caves and different geomorphological formations represent a paradise for cave explorers. The longest cave in Croatia is Medvednica in Ogulin (16,396 m long).

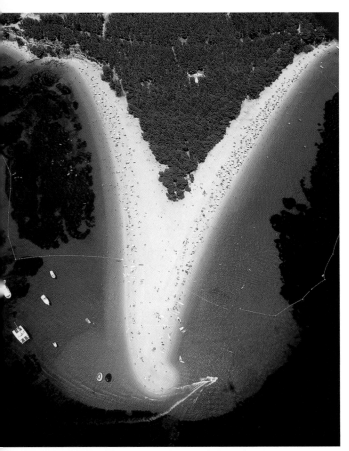

Well-known beach Zlatni rat (Golden Promontory) at Bol is a unique natural phenomenon

»THE COAST WITH A THOUSAND ISLANDS«

A unique natural feature of Croatia is its warm and cristal-clear sea (in the southern Adriatic, it is visible even 56 m deep and in the coastal area, the average visibility is 5 m). The Croatian part of the Adriatic is perhaps the most attractive one on the Mediterranean with picturesque islands, bays and magnificent beaches. The Adriatic is named after the town Adrii on the western coast (Greek adriati'ke thalassa, Latin - Mare Adriaticum) and is a total length of 7912 km. Out of this 74% (5.835.5 km) is the total coast, of this about 1778 km is the coast and about 4057 km (97,2%) are the islands. The rate of sea saltness is rather high, the average being about 38.3%. The central Dalmatian islands have a high insolation and are therefore suitable for winter holidays.

There are about 718 islands (60 of them are populated), 389 are rocks, 78 are ridges with numerous bays, channels, straits and with two large and many smaller peninsulas. The Croatian coast is considered one of the most attractive in Europe with an abundance of natural bays. Even in the international professional literature, such type of coast is often referred to as a »Dalmatian« one.

The peninsulas of Istria and Pelješac, the bay of Rijeka or the Kvarner bay, the Bakar bay, the Kaštela and the Gruž bays, the Novigrad and the Karin sea are all characterized by their size. The islands of Krk and Cres are the largest, then follow the islands of Brač, Hvar, Pag, Korčula, Dugi otok, Mljet, Hvar, Vis, Lošinj, Pašman, Šolta, Ugljan, Lastovo, Kornat, Čiovo, Olib, Molat, Vir, Murter, Iž etc. The highest island is the island of Brač (780 m high), then follow the islands of Cres (648 m high), Hvar (628 m high), Lošinj (589 m high), Vis (587 m high), Korčula (569 m high), Krk (568 m high), etc. The longest island is the island of Hvar (68 km long).

Rab, old town encompassed by walls

Pag, a town of stone in the protected cove turned towards the mainland

*Town of Hvar holds in its stone bosom precious
cultural and historical riches*

*Stari Grad, the oldest town on the island of
Hvar with valuable building heritage*

*Korčula, a town of monuments surrounded by walls
and towers has developed on a small peninsula*

*Town of Vis lies on the shores of the Vis Cove,
ancient Issa*

THE RIVERS AND LAKES

*»Flow the Sava, flow the Drava, not
even the Danube can take your power
Wide sea tell the world that the Croat
loves his people!«*

The rivers in Croatia empty either into the Black Sea (62%) or into the Adriatic (38%). The Sava, the longest river in Croatia flows towards the Black Sea (it is 940 km long with 556 km of it flowing through Croatia). Its larger tributories are: the Lonja and the Trebes (132 km) with the Česma or Čazma (123 km), the Kupa (296 km) together with the Dobra (104 km), the Korana (134 km), the Glina (100 km) and the Una (213 km, out of which 120 km through Croatia). Besides the Sava, there is the Bosut (186 km of which 143 km flows through Croatia). In the eastern part of Croatia, there flows the Danube (188 km in Croatia out of 2860 km) the second longest river in Europe. The Danube's tributaries are the Vuka (112 km) and, in the northern Pannonian part, the Drava river (305 km in Croatia out of 749 km) with the Bednja (133 km) etc.

Omiš, town at the impressive estuary of the Cetina River

The rivers which empty into the Adriatic are short in their flow but with high downfalls and are therefore rich in water and natural beauty. The largest rivers are: the Mirna in Istria (53 km), the Zrmanja in Dalmatia (69 km), the Krka (73 km), the Cetina (100 km) and the Neretva river (20 km in Croatia out of 213 km).

The karst rivers due to their chalk barriers and numerous waterfalls are especially attractive to tourists, particularly the Krka river which sinks into subterranean passages of chalk formation. Other subterranean rivers are: the Lika (78 km), the Gacka (55 km), the Mrežnica (62 km) and others. Some of them empty into the sea along the karst coast forming submarine springs.

The lakes in Croatia are scarce but they are rich in their beauty. The largest is the Vransko jezero near Biograd (the area of 30.2 square kilometers), then follow the Vransko Lake on the island of Cres (5.8 square kilometers), Prokljansko on the Krka river (11.5 square kilometers), the Baćin Lakes near Ploče (six lakes with the total area of 1.4 square kilometers), the lake Kuti or Đuvelek near Opuzen (1.3 square kilometers) etc.

The most famous are the Plitivice Lakes (16 lakes with a total area of 1.9 square kilometers). The artificial lakes were mainly created for the needs of the following hydro-electric power plants: Peruća (13 square kilometers) near Sinj, Krušćićko (3.9 square kilometers) near Gospić, Borovik (5 square kilometers) near Đakovo, Omladinsko or Lokvarsko (2.1 square kilometers), Bajer (0.5 square kilometers) near Delnice, Sabljačko (1.2 square kilometers) near Ogulin, etc. The Butoniga Lake near Motovun in Istria were created in order to supply the tourist resorts on the Istrian coast with fresh water.

There are also mineral springs used for the production of mineral water such as Jamnička and Lasinjska kiselica, Lipički studenac and the Kalnik (Apatovačka) mineral water.

Baćina Lakes, six mutually connected karst lakes

Imotski, Blue Lake, a geo-morphological natural monument

Islet of Visovac with the Franciscan Monastery amidst Lake Visovac on the Krka River

PEARLS OF NATURE

*T*he almost untouched nature in Croatia attracts numerous tourists.There are eight national parks (**Risnjak, the Plitivice Lakes, the Kornats, the island of Mljet, the islands of Brijuni, the Krka, Paklenica** and the **North Velebit**), ten parks of natural wilderness (the Velebit, the Biokovo, the Medvednica mountains, the Telašćica bay, the Kopački rit, the Lonjsko polje, Žumberak – Samoborsko gorje, the Papuk, Učka and Lake Vrana), two strictly protected areas (the **Hajdučki** and the **Rožanski kukovi** on the Velebit and the **White** and **Samrske rocks** on the Velika Kapela passage, 69 specially protected areas, 23 parks and forests, 28 specially protected areas and 72 parks of nature, i.e. (geographical, geological and paleontological, geomorphological areas and rare types of trees.); 14 gardens (parks, arboretums, botanical gardens or just single trees or the groups of them. The Plitivice Lakes are included in the UNESCO's list of World natural heritage.

In the dense forests of the mountainaous Croatia, there is the National park of the Plitivice Lakes or just the Plitivice Lakes which are outstanding in their beauty. The area of 419,479 hectars has the aboundannce of karst lakes (16), limestone barriers and different waterfalls and cascades. The lakes spread between Mala Kapela and the Plješivica 8 km long in the area of 2 square kilometers. The

Plitvice Lakes National Park, 16 lakes connected with numerous falls

Dense woods of birch and fir trees are the greatest value of the Risnjak National Park

Magnificent canyon in the Paklenica National Park

Brijuni National Park, islands covered with lush vegetation

High vertical rocks in the Velebit National Park

lakes are as follows (from the highest to the lowest ones): the Prošćansko Lake or the Prošće (636 m above the sea level), the Ciginovac, the Okrugljak, the Batinovac, the Vir, the Great and the Small lake, the Galovac, the Milino and the Gradinsko Lake, the Great Burget, the Kozjak, the Milanovac, the Gavranovac, the Kaluđerovac and the Novakovića Brod (502 m above the sea level). The largest and the deepest lakes are: the Kozjak (the area of about 82 hectars, 46 m deep) and the Prošćansko Lake (about 68 hectars and 37 m deep). The White and the Black rivers bring the largest volume of water to the lakes while near the Prošćansko Lake they merge with the main stream of water. The influx of water from the last lake joins the Korana river.

Among the natural attractions, there are the Sastavci or the Plitivice waterfall (70 m high) which thunder down to the lower lakes. This unique sight is framed by a dense wood of pine and beech-trees in the Čorkova Valley. The Golubnjača and the Šupljara caves along with the Black Cave are geomorphological phenomena of nature.

In Gorski Kotar, in the area of about 30 square kilometers, there is a national park called Risnjak (3.014 hectars), the living place of rare animals such as lynx, chamois, bear, black cock and other animals. There is a splendid view from the top of the Risnjak (1528 m) which in itself justifies the plans for an extension of the National park westward to Snježnik and northwards to the Kupa river.

Proclaimed in 1969, the **North Velebit** is the youngest Croatian national park. It is 145 km long and 1737 m high (Vaganski vrh). Because of its characteristics, especially its vegetation, it is the

Kornati National Park, the densest island group in the Mediterranean

most important Croatian mountain and a special symbol for all the Croats. It is mainly rocky on the coastal area but its interior is wooded and particularly interesting. Part of the Velebit near the sea is the National park Paklenica and the whole area is included in to the UNESCO's chart, the international network of protected areas of biosphere. The geomorphological phenomena are the Rožanski and Hajdučki kukovi (1,220 hectars) and the special area of woods called Štirovača (about 119 hectars). Other geomorphological phenomenon are the Cerovac caves which are 3.5 km long, situated along the Gračac-Knin road. Dabarski kukovi near the Oštarije passage, the Stapina, the Bojinac, the Tulove grede rocks and Luca's cavity (1392 m deep, the eighth deepest in the world) are particularly interesting. Lovers of mountaineering

can easily reach the attractive »Premužić's path, a passage which leads through Rožanski kukovi and to other paths and rocks. On the Velebit, there is a special botanical area called Zavižan-Balino-vac-Zavižanska kosa (118 hectars) and there is a botanical garden (about 50 hectars) in Modrić-dol, (1480 m above the sea level) near the weather station on Zavižan and the mountain lodge in Vučjak which can be also reached by the road.

Lička Plješivica with its primeval forest of pine and beech trees, the highest peak of the Velika Kapela and the area of Gorski kotar with its winter recreational centre at Bjelolasica (1533 m) are planned as future national parks. The karst relief of Velika Kapela includes the protected areas of White and Samarske Rocks (about 1,175 hectars). There are some strangely shaped rock towers be-

Krka National Park, magical world of falls

tween Bjelolasica and the White and Samarske rocks amongst the wooded area. There are roads leading from Jasenka to Mrkopalj and one passing over Begovo Razdolje, the highest village in Croatia (1078 m above the sea level).

In Baranja, there is a famous **Kopački rit** (about 17,770 hectars), a nesting place for many species of birds such as black stork, white heron, eagle and other rare species. It is also the largest spawning place for fish living in the Danube. The park is rich in wildlife such as deer, roe and boar and a part of it (7,000 hectars) has been proclaimed a protected zoological area.

The western part of the favourite Medvednica excursion place or the »Zagreb mountain« (22,826 hectars) is also considered a nature park and is also called »the lungs of Zagreb« due to its dense wood. The Lonja valley (50,650 hectars), the flooded area along the Sava river, is characterized by moorish vegetation and rich fauna.

Due to their rich animal and plant life, the Papuk, Žumberak and Samobor hills and part of the Zagorje region and the Mrežnica river with its limestone waterfalls, are included among the nature parks of Croatia.

In the coastal area there are several national parks such as Paklenica, Krka, the islands of Briuni, the Komats and the island of Mljet.

National park Paklenica (3,617 hectars) situated in the southern and coastal part of the Velebit is made up of maginficent eroded slopes - the valleys of Great and Small Paklenica. The area of Paklenica is 36 square kilometers wide and spans 20 to 1661 m of the high Crljeni peak with different flora and fauna (bears, wild cats, boars, martens, reptiles and birds). The most attractive part of the Great Paklenica park, not far from the Adriatic tourist road (about 3 km), is the high rock called the Anić rock, which is 400 m high and afavourite among mountainneers.

The Krka River (175 km) is a hydrological and morphological phenomenon of amazing beauty: there are seven limestone waterfalls from Knin to its estuary (the famous Skradinski buk and the Roški waterfall), several lakes (Prokljansko, Visovačko), etc. About two thirds of the stream flows through the national park (from the old fortresses of Nečven and Trošenj to the Šibenik bridge - 14,200 hectars). The national park area is rich in animal life, especially fish and birds, and in cultural and historical heritage (the ruins of the medieval forts of Trošenj, Nečven, Bogoćin, Kamičak, Ključica, the Franciscan monastery and the church on the Visovac islet, the monastery Krka/Aranđelovac).

In the vicinity, there is a special geomorphological and hydrological area (about 280 hectars) with the Krčić stream and the Topoljski waterfall (20 m high) which descends directly into the Krka river.

The islands of Brijuni (the area of 3,635 hectars) are the most interesting group of islands in Istria (14 islets) which are joined to the mainland by the shallow Fažana channel, (12 m deep). The largest islands are the Great (5.6 square kilometers) and the Small Brijuni (1 square kilometer). The Great Brijuni islands are characterized by their landscape of green grass. There is a Zoo, a »Safari« park and many cultural and historical monuments including Illyrian and Roman ruins in the Verige bay (the three temples, baths, villas from the first century, the Byzantine fort in the Dobrika bay and some sacred structures). The memorial museum is situated in the newly reconstructed palace. It is a distinguished tourist resort

Islet of St Mary in the middle of an island lake in the Mljet National Park

with hotels, beaches, golf and tennis playgrounds, hunting sites and paths for a small tourist train. It is also possible to hire a bicycle. The island can be reached by small tourist boats from Fažana.

The islands of Kornati are the most densly grouped islands in the Medeterranean with more than 140 islands, islets and rocks. There are four groups of islands: the so-called interior group or the Upper Kornat and the outside group or the Lower Kornat. There are three channels between them the Sitski, the Žutski and the Kornatski. The

National park consists of the Lower Kornat which has about a hundred islands and islets with exceptionally rich submarine life (22,375 hectars).

The largest island called Kornat (32.6 square kilometers) has the highest peak Metlina 235 m high), the largest settlement Vrulje and large fields such as Trtuša and Tarac where the Turet tower is situated (6th c.). Larger islands are Sit, Žut, Piškera (Jadra), Kurba Vela, Levrnaka and Lavsa. Especially interesting are the islets with their folk names such as Balun, Klobučar, Trbuh, Mrtvac, Golac, Baba, Kurbarić, Kurba (Vela and Mala), Tovar, Košara, Blitvica, Prduša, Babina guzica, Bludni rt etc.

Modern ACI marinas are situated on the islets of Žut and Piškara (120 moorings) which also has ruins dating from the Roman times. Murter is the most suitable starting point for excursions into the Kornati National Park.

The Mljet National Park (3,100 hectars) is situated on the western part of the same island. It is characterized by woods (more than 70% of the island) and by the Large Lake (145 hectars, 46 m deep) and the Small Lake (24 hectars, 29 m deep). The Large lake is linked by a channel (30 m long, 10 m wide and 2.5 m deep) with the Soline Bay and the open sea. The ruins of the ancient palace in Polače and the Benedictine monastery (12th c.) with St. Mary's church are situated on an islet in the Large Lake and are valuable cultural and historical monuments. Besides the well-maintained paths weaving through the woods, there is a paved road alongside the lakes leading to the bay of Soline.

Other nature parks are the Biokovo (19,550 hectars), the Telašćica (6,706 hectars) on Dugi otok (Long island), the Učka, the islands of Lastovo and Elafiti and the lower part of the Neretva river.

EASTERN AND CENTRAL CROATIA

*E*astern and central or the Pannonian Croatia is the largest part of Croatia with a total area of 54.4%, or 30,776 square kilometeres. This area is also the most populated with 66.4% or 3.175,000 of the inhabitants. The whole area is rich from an economic point of view (the so-called »cornfields« of Croatia, oil, hundred-year old oak trees, the international navigable waterway of the Danube, tourist resorts with numerous spas, hunting places, parks of nature etc.). This area is actually mainly the peri-Pannonian area because the Pannonian characteristcs are associated only with parts of Eastern Crtoatia, the so-called East-Croatian plain which includes Eastern Slavonia and Baranja and Western Srijem (the area from the western slopes of the Psunj and the Papuk mountains up to the western slopes of the Fruška gora). The western part of Eastern Croatia is characterized by smaller geographical units (Podravina, the Požega valley and Posavina). The central part of Croatia includes the Lonjsko-ilovska valley, Podravina by the Bilogora, the region of Hrvatsko zagorje, Podravina near Varaždin, Međimurje, Pokuplje, the area of Banovina and Kordun and the Zagreb urban area.The area between the Ilova, the Drava, the Sava and the Danube rivers is usually called Slavonia. In the Middle Ages until the Ottoman invasions, the name Slavonia refered to central Croatia and part of the Federation of Bosnia and Herzegovina.

MOUNTAINOUS CROATIA

*T*he mountains are the smallest area of Croatia (7912 square kilometers or 14% of the total area of Croatia). They are sparsely populated (144,000 inhabitants or 3% out of the total number of population and consist of a high karst area (more than 1000 m high) with subterranean and fluvial valleys. Due to some differences between the northern part (Gorski kotar-2350 square kilometers) and the southern one (Lika - 5562 square kilometers) both names are used i.e. the region of Lika and Gorski kotar.

The most famous part of mountainous Croatia and the jewel of the European tourist trade is the National park of the Plitvice lakes (under the UNESCO's protection as part of the world's heritage) which is situated along the Zagreb-Split motorway. There are excellent conditions for recreation and winter sports with well maintained skiing tracks in Platak (near the Adriatic sea), Bjelolasica, Delnice and Mrkopalj.

Gospić, winter idyll

MEDITERRANEAN CROATIA

*T*he Mediterranean part of Croatia consists of the region of Istria, the Croatian littoral and Dalmatia.

Istra is the largest peninsula (2820 square kilometers). It is divided according to the colour of soil, i.e. white Istria (poor in water and arable soil), grey Istria (hills with soft flish soil and the main rivers of the Dragonja, the Mirna and the Raša), red Istria (spacious karst valleys covered with fertile red soil).

The Croatian littoral or **the Kvarner** (3272 square kilometers) includes the narrow coastal line from the Preluk bay near Volovsko to the es-

tuary of the Zrmanja river and the islands of Cres, Lošinj, Krk, Rab and Pag and with the islets of Unije, Susak and Ilovik. It is called Kvarner after Kvarner Bay, the largest bay in the Adriatic.

Dalmatia is a historical name for the area south of the Croatian littoral. The notion of Dalmatia has changed over history. In the Roman times it included the area as far as Posavina, in the Middle Ages, it was reduced to the coastal towns and islands, whilst during the Venetian invasions in the seventeenth and eighteenth centuries, it extended to the coastal hinterland (Sinj, Knin, Imotski etc.). The »Kingdom of Dalmatia« under the Austrian rule, included

Pula, previous Roman colony, today a modern tourist town

Rijeka, town of past centuries, harmonious architecture and valuable monuments

Korzo, main walking area in Rijeka

the area between the island of Pag and the Zrmanja river as far as Spič, the northwestern suburb of Bar (today in Montenegro). Since the area south of the Prevlaka peninsula forms part of Montenegro with the borders changing after World War II, the present-day Dalmatia includes the area between Tribanj-Krušćica (community of Starigrad, 32 km far from Zadar), the Prevlaka peninsula, the sub-mediterranean hinterland (Zagora) and the islands (about 11,770 square kilometers). Depending upon its gravitational influence on larger towns, Dalmatia can be subregionally divided into the northern Dalmatia (Zadar and Šibenik), central Dalmatia (Split) and southern Dalmatia (Dubrovnik).

Makarska, tourist centre of the Makarska Riviera below the craggy Biokovo

Cavtat, historical, cultural and tourist centre of Konavle

CONTENTS